A LEGACY RESTATED

A Legacy Restated

The Work of Bernhard Behrens

Four Essays with Current-day Reviews

Edited by

Christopher Houghton Budd

SteinerBooks | 2024

2024
STEINERBOOKS
An imprint of Anthroposophic Press, Inc.
834 Main Street, PO Box 358
Spencertown, New York 12165
www.steinerbooks.org

LIBRARY OF CONGRESS CONTROL NUMBER: 2024945072

ISBN: 978-1-62148-381-6

Contents

The person acting is always without conscience;
none has conscience but the person observing.

– GOETHE

Bernhard Behrens's Legacy

This anthology has seen the light of day by chance, as it were. There was no initial strategy in the decision to do it, which began with a suggestion by Swiss economist and Waldorf teacher, Fionn Meier, and there is none in its publishing other than, important as it is, to see if, when published, it confirms Fionn's sense that it is relevant to today. Little known in the English-speaking world, Bernhard Behrens's work has stayed in the background of the social sciences in the Anthroposophical Movement for many a long year, also in Germany. It was taken off the shelf, as it were, dusted off, and reviewed in Germany in 2023 by Manfred Kannenberg and Ralf Neff, in a collection called *Anthroposophically Oriented Economics.*[1] Those texts, which are available only in German and are not included or replicated here, were titled:

Four Introductory Studies (Vier einführende Studien)

---

1 *Anthroposophisch orientierte Wirtschaftswissenschaft. Eine Studienreihe—1930–32.* Eds. Ralf Neff and Manfred Kannenberg. Verlag Ch. Möllmann, Borchen, Germany, 2023.

> *The True Relationship of World Economy to National Economy*[2] (Die wahre Beziehung der Weltwirtschaft zur Volkswirtschaft)
> *Capital Formation, Transfer and Management in Relationship to Price Formation* (Kapitalbildung, Kapitalübertragung u. Kapitalverwaltung in ihrer Beziehung zur Preisbildung)
> *The Change in Direction of Economic Endeavors in the 20th Century* (Der Richtungswechsel des Wirtschaftsstrebens im 20. Jahrhundert).

Reviewed by Hans Erhard Lauer in 1930 and more recently commented on by Helmut Woll (see chapter 2), we trust these accounts will give the reader a sense of Behrens's understanding of Rudolf Steiner's contribution to economics. The recent republication of his essays also included an introduction by Virginia Sease, to whom we owe a debt. As a citizen of the United States, the details provided by her appraisal give an "insider's" sense of Behrens's biography during his time in London, Canada and the United States. This backgrounding is followed by Fionn's assessment of Behrens's relevance today (chapter 3), as illustrated in the four booklets

---

2   This is a delicate matter. In English, for better or worse, since Alfred Marshall, political economy is today called economics and economics is primarily nation-state based. So national economy has been used here to emphasize the point that we need to step from nation state economies into a single world economy. —Ed. (Note: Not all editorial comments are seamless. For this reason, with the exception of those in chapter 5, certain footnotes are prefaced by the initials of their authors, signaling that not all such comments are or need to be agreed to by everyone. Most such commentary is uncontentious, although certain of the remarks denoted with CHB may raise eyebrows. They are not ill-meant or polemical, however, but intended to protect Behrens's expositions from the challenges they will be subject to today if his arguments are not given the wider context they merit. Those footnotes belonging to general editorship are denoted "—ED." or left blank.)

reproduced here (chapter 6–9), which were originally published in the United States when the 1940s gave way to the
1950s:

> Conditions vital to the Social Organism
> *(Anthroposophic Press, 1944)*
> The Economic Essentials of Spiritual Life.
> *(Anthroposophic Press, 1945)*
> Goethe and the Social Question.
> (Voluntas Press, Los Angeles, 1951)
> Death and Life of Democracy.
> (Voluntas Press, Los Angeles, 1951)

They were overall edited by economic and monetary historian Christopher Houghton Budd (chapter 1), but sepa-
rately reviewed. First by Fionn Meier (chapter 3), whose idea
it was to make Behrens's work available afresh. Then comes
my own, admittedly tough, assessment (chapter 4), followed
by Stephen Vallus, who as a citizen of the United States gets
the last word (chapter 5).[3]

Each of the three commentaries was written from a
current but different perspective, therefore. Fionn Meier is
a young Swiss economist and "threefolding" activist well
versed in monetary affairs. My own contribution is written
as an economic and monetary historian. Though English, I
have had a lifelong relationship with the United States, dating back to my teens. I do not have the familiarity of a true
citizen of that country, but nor is my acquaintance as cur-
sory as Fionn's has been to date. Stephen Vallus, on the other
hand, is a United States citizen by birth, equally aware of the
threefold nature of social life and world economic matters,

---

3   All three commentators are colleagues in the Economics Conference
     of the Goetheanum (economics.goetheanum.org), the work of which
     provides the context for this publication.

and a long-time practitioner in United States tax accounting. He shares why, in his view, his country more than any other ought to revisit Bernhard Behrens's work.

Between the three of us we do not pretend to have all bases covered; indeed, one reason for publishing is to invite others to engage with this material—for it is a very long way from the early 1950s to today. Folks like Stephen and myself stepped onto the earth's stage way back then. As we get ready to step off, it is interesting to ponder who is now showing up. Of the three of us, of course, only Fionn will likely be able to welcome them and provide a living link!

One thing is sure: this is a must-read for "threefolders" of all ages and stripes. And the whole "event" is made felicitous by Behrens's proficient English.[4] To use a somewhat ugly but well-intended expression, if we recommend taking a fresh, and for some a new, look at Behrens's work, it is because we are following up on what the "triangulated data" of our essays points to. Although written blind to one another, taken together our three assessments are of one overall encouraging voice. The challenge, as ever, will be that what Behrens describes and, indeed, advocates does not lend itself to today's generally binary mindset, especially in the aspic halls of academia. Understand his message, however, and one will be compelled to social scientific action, and so to supply what one considers to be absent.

≈

That said, there are a number of matters we would like to draw attention to concerning how this work is likely to sit in an English-speaking and non-anthroposophical world. First,

---

4   From its various imperfections and over-liberal use of the definite pronoun, we assume it was not translated. —Ed.

how altogether does anthroposophy and Rudolf Steiner's work in general interface with the innate spiritual culture, traditions and sensibilities of the United States, with its primarily Anglo-Saxon and outwardly Christian biases, despite the wide diversity of its citizens?[5] For example, there are quite a number of, often sudden and possibly insurmountable, anthroposophical references (*inter alia*, the three "I"s, Michael and the Christ Event[6]) that, lacking explanation, might prevent important parts of these texts from reaching an ecumenical readership. One can, of course, argue that the threefold social order is not to be divorced from anthroposophy, and yet moral tact is never to be forgotten. Rudolf Steiner himself said,

> The universally human character striven for in the Waldorf School [, for example,] cannot be too strongly emphasized. One can say in a case like this that a person who is a genuine anthroposophist is not in the least concerned with the name anthroposophy; he is concerned with what it is about [which is] universally human concerns. So when it is brought to bear on a certain goal, it can function only in the most universally human sense.... It is contrary to the nature of anthroposophy to do this. Anthroposophy can only give rise to universally human institutions; that is what comes naturally to it.[7]

---

5   And, some would say, the clearly unchristian nature of some of its behaviors. —ED.

6   Not to mention, "the supreme World Spirit, by revealing Himself in the form of an idea, takes up His abode in the Holy of Holies of His temple built by Him" and "the Idea as the Word (Logos) of the eternal Spirit" in *Goethe and the Social Question* or "the abyss of perdition" in *Conditions Vital to the Social Organism*—and many overtly anthroposophical references, which presuppose substantial familiarity with Steiner's wider *oeuvre*. —ED.

7   *Awakening to Community*, Anthroposophic Press, New York 1974,

And, indeed, neither his book on the threefold nature of social life, nor the contents of the lectures at the 1922 West–East Congress mention anthroposophy.[8] The threefold nature of the human organism keeps the faith well enough, and in this editing we have followed suit. As Behrens wrote: "The 'particular,' that is, the individual human being, can only be considered as a threefold entity composed of body, soul and spirit. As soon as man is recognized as such an entity, the general form of the social organism and its laws will also be recognized."[9]

Second, while English-speaking people may not be individually complicit with the world's seemingly orchestrated refusal of Rudolf Steiner's social ideas, they nevertheless inhabit a world predicated on precisely that. The air we breathe, our daily news, our governments' continuous policies—what else is behind them but to silence or stop up the ears of English-speaking citizens and subjects by locking our minds on to the bifurcation of left or right, capitalism

---

Lecture 1. CW 257.

8   *The Tension between East and West,* revised 2nd edition, Steinerbooks, New York, 2024 (CW 83).

9   It is important not to forget here the hugely under-estimated and under-credited significance of Rudolf Steiner's discovery of the threefold nature of the human being, which ranks with William Harvey's discovery of the circulation of the blood (not to be seen as synonymous with the heart as a pump). When Behrens predicated his social science on the threefold human organism, he must have known full well what he was doing, for that is also the basis of Rudolf Steiner's 1919 book, *Die Kernpunkte der Sozialen Frage,* variously translated in English but here referred to as *The Threefold Nature of Social Life,* rather than the more common but static *Threefold Social Order.* This choice reinforces Steiner's research into just that matter: namely, the threefold nature of social life reflects and reinforces the threefold nature of the human being, but it does not precede it. It is as if, causatively speaking, society is a reflection of man; man is not a reflection of society. Society did not come first. —ED.

or communism? Thereby, never calling on our own I as the author and arbiter of social conduct, we do not have enough occasion to replace binary thinking with trinary, which is the key to understanding and arriving within the inner logic of threefolding ideas.

Thirdly, much has happened since the 1950s when Bernhard Behrens was alive. The United States is not what it was then: cocksure of itself and proud of its Manhattan Project, yet given to the kind of anti-communist witch-hunts that lay behind McCarthyism and the prosecution of the Rosenbergs, for example. And then there is the question of how Behrens was related to the mores of his time. There are times when he writes in a tone that puts one in mind of those who nowadays would "make America great again." For example, there are a number of places where he speaks of "Americans" as if he only has in mind those who are known, albeit colloquially and somewhat derogatorily, as "wasps"—white northern European, even white Anglo-Saxon protestant. A Latino, an Afro-American or an indigenous "First Nation" person would likely be offended by his ignoring them; not only now in our more "awake" times, but also back then. Likewise, concerning Asian folk, he writes as if they do not seek liberty and prosperity or do not have every right to do so as those who hail from Europe. It is surely not meant to come across that way; even so, today's sensibilities warrant something of a reader's advisory in this regard.

Throughout, we have substituted terms that we thought were not precise to the English ear, especially the English constitutional ear. We eschewed "legal system" in favor of "rights life," for example, because "life" resonates better than system, but also on the grounds that, while rights includes law, the reverse does not necessarily hold. That said, reference to rights life is unusual, though not archaic, and carries the nuance that Steiner does not mean by it the very different idea of human rights associated with Theodore, Franklin, and Eleanor Roosevelt.

It is also the case that in normal parlance, one does not speak of economic life outside the anthroposophical movement. Paradoxically, perhaps, one can speak readily enough of spiritual life; this rolls off the tongue without causing alarm or offence or drawing attention to itself. But "rights life" and "economic life" can rarely be used without eliciting a frisson of concern: the feeling, even fear, that something is *meant* by these terms; entailing an agenda of some kind, or, worse yet, a challenging social conception. People prefer "law," "legal," or "politics," even though these, when thought about, are subsets of a larger realm and not a match for it as a whole. And they prefer the dead abstraction "economy" to anything that portends life and living. When speaking in public life in English, one has to know this and know how to manage it.

More subtly, preferring law over rights can be a giveaway for a shift from self-moralizing to being externally moralized; meaning, having an idea about how others should and should be encouraged, if not made, to behave. Where, at times Behrens seems close to saying, "let's make America great again," this may simply be due to the impression one gets of him being somewhat strait-laced and of his time, a time when men provided for families, when everyone went to school then college, and when all lived a happy Lucille and Desi kind of life—provided, of course, that for the most part one was white and middle class.

We have left the terms "mankind," "man," "brother," "father," "fraternity" alone, on the excuse that that is how Behrens wrote and that in his day such terms—thought by many today to have overtones of male supremacy—were not thought (by those who used them) to be a problem. On the other hand, we have changed "supra-national" to "universal" in order to avoid confusion with "super-national." And "America," and in places also "North America," has been substituted with "United States," partly in deference to the growing sensitivities of those who live in the Americas but not in the United States, but also because, although Behrens lived in Canada for a period, his writings are about the United States.[10] Moreover, it is not possible to equate the development of the United States with or transpose it to Canada. Indeed, our treatment of "North America" warrants some explanation, in that a European perspective can place an emphasis on the destinies and aspirations of those, such as Continental and Irish European emigrés, who often went there in exile or in flight. Equally important and informative, however, if not more so in both the cases of the United States and Canada, is the history in link with Great Britain and its constitutional monarchy (e.g., "no taxation without representation") and its settlement activities. In both countries today, these have resulted in the Anglo-Saxons having roles and possibilities "superior" to anyone else. One also has to evaluate the North America story in terms of still-active Masonic culture, the karma of the "first peoples," the growing Hispanic population (with Spanish expected to be the major language in the United States in the not too distant future), and, of course, the experience of those brought

---

10   A viable and readily adopted alternative might be the United States of North America. —ED.

from Africa. Also in today's mix is Rapturist ideology and the Zionist movement, both very strong in the United States especially.

Understandably, perhaps, little if any of this figures in either what Steiner or Behrens said, but it will be something today's readership will likely be very fast to point out and for which, therefore, one has to have a prepared, coherent, viable and anthroposophically true response. This may not have been so crucial at the time of the 1922 West–East Congress, where Rudolf Steiner speaks about the Europe-America connection, but it is inescapable today. One has also to be very clear where Canada stands in Rudolf Steiner's image, because Canada's history is not that of the United States and takes one also into the role of France in the North American story. Interesting, too, is Steiner's overarching use of "Western."

Next, addressing a well-known translator's conundrum when it comes to Steiner in English, does one use "spiritual life," which is a bit "in your face," or the less challenging (because less meaningful) "cultural life"? Or does one use them randomly, hopping from one to the other as if unsure whether they are, or one means them to be, synonyms? In deference to anthroposophical authenticity, for the most part, we have opted for spiritual life and consistency.

At a more technical level, when relevant to do so, "non-compensatory income" has taken the place of Behrens's use of "unearned income," since the latter term is already spoken for in modern finance, meaning interest and dividend receipts. Likewise, for those who receive loans, "borrowers" is more normal (and less loaded) than "debtors." "Creditors" are also often renamed "lenders."

It is important to let the reader know that overall the editorial commentaries are not seamless. In particular, a Continental European interpretation such as Behrens would make can give to law a primary significance that an Anglo-Saxon will not recognize. This is important because the rights life of the United States is largely derived from Britain, whether from the constitutional monarchy that was stepped away from or *The Rights of Man* and other works by Thomas Paine (from England), which made this step possible. The role and effect of equity underpinning and qualifying rights, for example, is evident in the maxim that "he who comes to court must come with clean hands." Or that a law, even if democratically promulgated, may still be unlawful. On the other hand, the idea of democracy and the valuing of that idea, as Behrens points out, belong to spiritual life and in that sense are universal, although the way democracy is given effect is national or folk-soul based. Here one has also to be especially mindful that "Western" democracy is problematical in that (a) its bi-party construct is an untruth, and (b) its proponents think it is universal. Moreover, dividing the world into left or right, capitalism or communism, etc. is a device as if designed to prevent the centering role of the I.

An unexpected, and unexplored, thought arose when in Fionn's review he suggested that the ideals of liberty, democracy and a depoliticized economic life need to be reborn (echoing my own "rebooted"), by which he means enlivened, from an anthroposophical point of view. Though not part of Fionn's intention, this opens up the prospect of anthroposophy or spiritual science[11] having a John the

---

11 In English, where the words *spirit* and *science* do not naturally
    occur together, one is tempted to say "true science." Also because

Baptist relationship to the social sciences. That an idea such as democracy, which goes back to Ancient Greek times and arose before the Christ Event, awaits and requires to have its shoes unlaced, perhaps in the sense that Thomas Aquinas "christened" the works of Aristotle.

Finally, there is Behrens's reference to Goethe. Predictable one might say, because of his German heritage and anthroposophical interests, but the link to Goethe is important also because it is Goethe who, per Wolf Franck writing in the spring of 1951, was "the man who expressed [a] Faustian longing for America..."[12] As a closing remark, this makes all the more interesting the fact, according to Bernd Hamacher, that Goethe owned a remnant of the mast of Columbus's ship—a father's reward for his thirst for knowledge.[13]

—*Christopher Houghton Budd, May 2024*

---

much that goes by the claim of natural science is not in fact truly scientific—and by its own yardstick. That said, the appellation "spiritual science" has been kept throughout. —ED.

12 "Goethe for America," Wolf Franck, in *The American Scholar*. The Phi Beta Kappa Society, Vol. 20, No. 2 (spring 1951), pp. 206–214. See: https://www.jstor.org/stable/41205395.

13 Writing in *Goethe and Money—the writer and modern economics*. Freier Deustche Hochschrift, Frankfurt, Germany 2012, p. 126.

2

Some Biography

B orn in Hamburg in 1892, Bernhard Behrens was an early advocate of associative economics. He understood well Rudolf Steiner's ideas about the threefold nature of social life, concerning which he was ever insightful, passionate and articulate—as this publication attests. Immediately prior to World War Two, events in Germany obliged him to leave (with his wife) for London, after which he went via Canada to the United States in 1941, where he was interned in Los Angeles until the end of the Second World War. Few other biographical details are to be found, except perhaps where, in *Death and Life of Democracy,* Behrens refers to "we in the United States." Perhaps this betokens citizenship; certainly identification. Little else seems known about him or what he did, but a background in business and social science seems certain. He died January 20, 1952.

That said, in a recent appraisal of Bernhard Behrens's work,[14] Dr. Helmut Woll of Germany's Institute for Contemporary Social Issues (Institut für soziale Gegenwartsfragen) provides some interesting observations. His perspective is presented here in abridged paraphrasing by Christopher Houghton Budd.

---

14 "Der freie Mensch verwandelt die Wirtschaft," in *Das Goetheanum,* No. 49/2023.

Before leaving Germany, Behrens published a seven-volume series on "anthroposophically oriented economics." These studies do not begin, as would be normal in economics, with the topics of demand, scarcity, and the need for a price system[15] and then end with global economic problems, but with Rudolf Steiner's fundamental social law: "The well-being of a community of people working together will be the greater, the less the individual claims for himself the proceeds of his work; that is, the more of these proceeds he makes over to his fellow workers, and the more his own needs are satisfied, not as the result of his own work but as the result of the work done by others."[16] Global economic questions then follow. Behrens reins in economic theory from behind, basing his approach not, as usual, on scientific methods, models and statistical procedures, but on Rudolf Steiner's *Philosophy of Freedom*.[17] Why not? And yet, what is the gain in knowledge from such an unconventional approach?

Behrens rightly places the free human spirit at the center of his considerations and thus clearly distances himself from *homo oeconomicus*, a concept that cannot provide a comprehensive explanation of economic events because it does not address the spiritual dimension of human existence. "We must now add another insight to this in order to reveal how the core part of Steiner's philosophy [the spirituality of the human being—Ed.] can be placed in direct relationship to

---

15 Echoing the standard trope: Resources are scarce. How does one allocate scarce resources? By the price mechanism. —ED.

16 First published 1905 in *Spiritual Science and the Social Question*. A three-part essay originally published in *Luzifer Gnosis,* 1905, part 3 (CW 34).

17 *The Philosophy of Freedom*, Rudolf Steiner Press, London 1972. Interestingly, Woll equates this philosophy directly with "spiritual science." —ED.

social life by serving to raise awareness of the true nature of economic association. Actually, it is astonishing how little it has been recognized so far that this is the actual starting point for a true awareness of real human communities and thus also economic association."

The idea (and fact) of our free spirit metamorphoses the traditional concepts of economics such as commodity, money, value and credit, into an associative economic framework that, by not thinking in terms of commodity and money "fetishes," opens the way to the question of true and fair values and prices. The alienation of work and the question of ownership can also be solved theoretically in this way. Likewise, the commodity character of work and land can be repudiated. In addition, while conventional economics neglects the consumer and leaves macroeconomic coordination to an anonymous market in a dysfunctional state, associative economics places the emphasis elsewhere. For example, "it [has] to be shown not only that consumption must determine the extent and intensity of overall economic production, [otherwise] the proper structure and regulation of money is not possible."

This approach only works for those readers who are prepared to deal with anthroposophical questions. This is not possible in normal economics, where one works with clearly defined terms, causal analytical models and statistical evidence. These are deliberately not provided by Behrens. Instead, he directs our attention to Steiner's books, *The Philosophy of Freedom* and *The Threefold Nature of Social Life*,[18] and his lectures on economics,[19] which are predicated on or provide

18 *The Threefold Social Order*, Oxford 1922. New Economy Publications, Canterbury, England 1996. CW 23.

19 Rudolf Steiner, *Economics: The World as One Economy* (CW 340),

the predicate for a successful combination of free spiritual life, equal rights life and fraternal economic life. "The spiritual origin of an association[20] should be made conscious as well as the social conditions within which associative economic life takes shape. This is just one aspect.... A second one opens up when one pays attention to the relationship that associative life has to the rights life, the community *qua* state. And a third consideration is required to show the effectiveness of an associative structure of the overall economy for fair pricing and value formation."

The content of Behrens's explanations is very condensed and requires a lot of prior knowledge of the humanities in the fields of economics and philosophy and a willingness to engage intensively with Behrens's booklets. Additional study of Rudolf Steiner's underlying writings is also required to do justice to this subject matter, the originals of which Bernhard Behrens delved deeply into, editing them confidently and independently. That this is about more than a new economic approach is very clear, while the grounds given by Behrens for free spiritual life and his statements about a prospective rights life in an associative economy make for remarkable reading.

≈

Anthroposophically Oriented Economics provides further insights into who Bernhard Behrens was and what he was about. It includes the following review from 1930 by

---

New Economy Publications, Canterbury, UK, 2014 [1996/1922]; also, *Rethinking Economics: Lectures and Seminars on World Economics* (CW 340–341), SteinerBooks, 2013.

20 Referring to Steiner's concept of economic life organized in associations, discussed by Behrens in due course. —Ed.

Hans Erhard Lauer, published in *Das Goetheanum*, No. 31, August 3, 1930:[21]

> I would like to point to an anthroposophical-scientific work that I believe should be warmly welcomed. It is a processing of Rudolf Steiner's economics course—which has long been more or less fallow—and which Bernhard Behrens has recently begun to publish in on-going editions under the title *Anthroposophically Oriented Economics*.[22] The publication emerges from economic studies that the author has been leading for years within the anthroposophical seminar in Hamburg founded by Louis Werbeck. So far two editions have been issued. And one can expect the best for the sequels, because what they offer is exemplary. The commentary mainly follows the economics course; however, the relevant representations from the *The Threefold Nature of Social Life*[23] and from social science are also happily presented.
>
> Rudolf Steiner's lectures have been reviewed in a fruitful way along with the then-economic literature. From this, the author builds a completely new economic theory on a broad basis, whose philosophical and methodological foundation is extremely solid. His thought process is of strict consistency and great clarity.
>
> The first issue provides the initial anthroposophical foundation. Economics is part of the social sciences and as such stands in the middle between natural scientific research and today's humanities. As a social science, it examines the nature of the relationship between people, in particular as regards their exchange of goods or services, which is the essential phenomenon of today's economic life. The price formation that arises through

---

21 Rendered into English by CHB.

22 *Anthroposophisch Orientierte Wirtschaftswissenschaft*, op. cit.

23 See footnote 9.

the use of money as a medium of exchange is, so to speak, the thermometer for the health or otherwise of economic conditions. The main task of economics is therefore to recognize how the working of the various factors in economic life ultimately results determinatively in the structuring of prices.

In order to address this, the second issue first provides an overview of the entire area and boundaries of the economy. It shows how economic life touches nature, on the one hand, and on the rights life and spiritual life on the other. Then the most important factors active in it are described, such as land, labor and capital. Their various interactions result in two main groups of products: those that are more nature-determined as in agriculture and those that are more capital-determined as in industry. Creating a balance between the two is the real task of trading.[24]

That is the thought process of the publications so far. Perhaps, in order to make the revolutionary significance of the new view more apparent, the author could have used conventional ideas more as a foil in some places. For instance, where he shows that needs must arise from spiritual life—whereas today they are not only satisfied by the economy, but also created by it. Or where he demonstrates that work as such has no economic value, but only gains value through its use for production that serves needs—whereas all of today's

---

24 CHB: How real is it to distinguish between agricultural and industrial products? Of course, there is a difference, but it is not one that Rudolf Steiner makes, in the sense that it is not his distinction between Value 1 (labor working on land) and Value 2 (labor organized by intelligence). This distinction does not follow through to goods, because all goods, whether food or machines, are the result of Value 1 and Value 2. Both owe their existence to the organization of labor; both owe their physical content to land (which is arguably the closest match in economics to Steiner's "Natur").

economic practice is characterized by the failure to take this fundamental truth into account.

Perhaps the subsequent editions will provide an opportunity for such information. In any case, we would like to wish the publication the widest possible distribution. After all, economic life is not an area for merely learned specialist interests. It concerns everyone. Not just in the general sense that everyone is within it as a producer or consumer, but also in the special sense that today—due to the division of labor—everything that anyone does economically has its meaning and consequences not just for oneself, but for the entire economic process. Becoming aware of the conditions for life and health in the economy is, therefore, not just a private and theoretical matter today, but a social demand and the first practical step towards improving the world economic situation, which is currently sinking ever deeper into a general crisis.

3

Behrens's Relevance
to the Social Question

Fionn Meier

At the end of his public endeavor for the threefold social organism, Rudolf Steiner spoke in June 1922 at the West–East Congress in Vienna about the importance of a spiritual collaboration between Europe and America. Only through this will the social challenges of our times be mastered:

> We must again find the possibility to speak philosophically out of a spirit that affects everyone, from the most uneducated to the most educated. In this way we can work together, think together, feel together, will together in establishing social prospects in the present but for the future. That will happen if an understanding can be brought about between the new seeds in Europe, as they have been described these days, and what is emerging in America, I would like to say, even at a higher level of culture among educated people in general. An understanding that will bring to the West the ground for a Western understanding of spiritual development. If we as Western people show ourselves capable of conceiving something spiritual out of what we grasp inwardly

within ourselves, and counter the Oriental spirit, which today is in a state of decadence, with a European-American spirit—then only will world economy and world trade as they exist today become possible on a basis of genuine trust between people.

—*Rudolf Steiner, 10 June 1922, CW 83*[25]

Today, Europe and America are still considered to be the place where the modern ideas of liberty, democracy and an economic life free of governmental interference have their origin and shared home. However, more and more signs show that this home is in danger of falling apart. Not primarily because of threats from outside, but because the inner core of these impulses, which are idealistic and human in their essence, have been almost destroyed by materialism and egotism. Where, therefore, are the sources that can lead to a rebirth of liberty, democracy, and a depoliticized economic life?

Bernhard Behrens's life can be seen in the light of the task of finding these sources and sharing them in the hope of a European-American collaboration towards a renaissance of these Western ideals. Behrens was born in Hamburg and lived there until, because of the Second World War, he left Germany, going first to England in 1939 and then to Canada and on to the United States in 1941.

It is hardly an exaggeration to state that Behrens was the first "anthroposophical economist." By 1930, he had published the series of articles on economics referred to in chapter 2, which show that he had a deep and profound

---

25 CHB: This raises a question: Given that the United States is a predominately Anglo-Saxon culture, where do England and things English figure in Steiner's assessment? In what sense, per Steiner, does Europe include England with her "appended" United States?

knowledge of the economics course given by Steiner in July and August 1922, as well as the economic literature of the time. In very clear lines of thought, he shows the contribution Rudolf Steiner made to topics central to economics—such as the price problem, the issues linked to economic globalization, and the question of credit.

In all his articles, Behrens shows that at the core of Steiner's contribution is what one might call the "anthroposophical turn" in economics. In essence, this means bringing the human being—not as an abstract *homo economicus*, but as a true human being consisting of body, soul and spirit—into economics, but without undermining its scientific foundation.

It is a striking symptom that Behrens's further destiny took him to the United States exactly the year when Paul Samuelson finished his doctoral thesis at Harvard, which eventually became the basis of almost all university textbooks on economics worldwide.[26] Samuelson's approach is entirely based on egotism and materialism, and thereby excludes any notion of the human being as a free spiritual being.[27]

Behrens's later writings in the United States take into account the special cultural, historical and geographical situation of that part of the world. It is to the United States especially that people from Europe went to live in *liberty*. It is also the United States that stands for the idea that it is a

---

26 *Foundations of Analytical Economics*, Paul A. Samuelson, first published 1947.

27 Concerning Samuelson, a 2007 critique by Arjo Klamer, Diedre McCloskey and Stephen Ziliak: *Is There Life after Samuelson's Economics? Changing the Textbooks*. Post Autistic Economics Review, May 2007—makes for interesting reading. As "post autistic" economists, they implicitly describe Samuelson as autistic and say it is time he either moved on or shared the stage with a wider range of views. Quite what "autism" means from a spiritual scientific perspective, however, may warrant debating.

universal human right not to be governed by autocrats, but to be free and able to decide *together as equals* via a democratic process the laws that regulate social life.[28] And it is in the United States where so many have sought to establish an *economic life* completely free of governmental interference.

It is evident that these three different fields or strivings not only exist within the social life of the United States especially, but are linked directly to the idea of the threefold nature of society that Rudolf Steiner described at the beginning of the 20th century in Continental Europe and Great Britain. For a Central European person (like myself) who knows about the threefold nature of social life, Behrens's writings can be an eye-opener as to how these ideas fit into his adopted country's history and culture.

Behrens places quite an emphasis on the most important issue for the future of the United States in particular: the need to find a truer understanding of what "liberty" means and entails, and by extension, the economic consequences involved in a more profound understanding of liberty. His writings also attempt to show the seeds that have grown in parts of Europe towards a similar deeper understanding of liberty, an idea that rests on the *experience* that spiritual activity (which starts from thinking in its higher expressions of imagination, inspiration, and intuition) is not separated

---

28   CHB: The question of autocracy reads differently on the Continent than in England and therefore the United States, insofar as that country's birth arose by distancing itself from the England of George III. By then, England had already disposed of autocratic governance, the very overthrow of which resulted in its version of constitutional monarchy. It was not until the First World War, with the demise of the Austro-Hungarian empire, that autocracy finally left the field on the Continent—until, that is, one remembers the true nature of Sovietism and the examples afforded by Stalin, Hitler, Salazar, and Franco, to mention only those belonging to Europe.

from the world, and that the inner essence of nature also reveals itself through this activity. This experience is the background of Goethe's artistic and scientific work. Rudolf Steiner further showed how this spiritual activity leads towards a true liberty of the human being and that, in drawing the social consequences of acknowledging the free spirit within the human being, Europe and America share a common task and destiny.

Towards the end of the Second World War, Behrens specified these consequences in the group of articles republished here, in which he outlined the deeper meaning of the free spirit and its consequences for democracy and economic life.

The United States has not yet managed to let ray forth a culture towards the rest of the world that gives the impression of a free spirit at work creating a new culture based on individual human destiny and creativity. Instead, it seems to fall either into spiritual dementia or isolationism.[29] Although Bernhard Behrens's writings are now more than fifty years old, what he has written is still at the core of today's social problems. If studied today, they are likely to make an essential contribution to the healthy development of the seeds of Europe and the strivings of the United States in the tasks before us—of strengthening the unfolding of a society based on liberty and equality, and eventually also creating a world-wide economic life in the service of humanity.

---

29 FM: Judging by the two potential candidates for the 2024 presidential elections, for example.

4

Bernhard Behrens 75 Years On

Christopher Houghton Budd

I first "met" Bernhard Behrens in the early 1970s on my initial reading of Rudolf Steiner's The Social Future lectures,[30] where in the 1945 Anthroposophic Press edition he had provided some valuable extra and explicative commentary.[31] "Here," I thought, "is a good social scientific mind." I often had recourse to his remarks but left them largely unmentioned and untouched until 2009, when the annual meeting of the Economics Conference of the Goetheanum took as its theme: Economic Life at the Threshold—Associative Economics in the 21st Century. My own contribution to that gathering and the subsequent book that emerged[32] brought Behrens back on the radar (or mine, at least). Only recently, in reading the four pamphlets included in this anthology, did I sense his might also be an entrepreneur's pen. Even so, my initial acquaintance and subsequent deepening of his work

---

30 Rudolf Steiner, *The Social Future: Culture, Equality, and the Economy*, SteinerBooks, Great Barrington, MA, 2013 [1919].

31 On "the associative and company principles" and on Steiner's ideas concerning so-called expenditure taxation.

32 *Towards True Pricing and True Income. 2009 Economics Conference Proceedings*. Search aeBookstore.com.

occurred blind to who he was, apart from a German person translocated to the United States, to what he did in life, and to where he belonged. I also remained ignorant of this throughout the writing of this essay, which entirely preceded my overall commentary and was written without sight of my colleagues' contributions. (The details in chapter 3 arrived subsequently.)

This not knowing the author approximates the method and virtue of blind peer review. Certainly, in this case, with no biographical information and even though I only have these fragments to go on, it is clear that, whoever Bernhard Behrens was, he writes not only perceptively, but also with insight. On this basis alone I recommend his texts be read, but I suggest one does so in the sequence of *Goethe and the Social Question, Conditions Vital to the Social Organism, Death and Life of Democracy*, and *The Economic Essentials of Spiritual Life*, because the latter three flow from the first, which in itself is both a clear exercise in social scientific thinking, while his treatment of Goethe, if in places flawed or at least incomplete, is as succinct (and Anglo-Saxon) an introduction to him as one could wish for. As is also his mapping from Goethe to Steiner. It even feels as if the "true" thread of modern Germany's post-Goethe evolution is being tracked here, both historically and autobiographically. Behren's treatment in the Goethe essay of threefold social ordering as a reflection of our own threefold organism is also elegant and precise.[33]

The essays brought together here can be read individually, of course, and, my earlier advice notwithstanding, in

---

33 For these reasons, they are also presented in that sequence here, even at risk of not being able to follow the chronology of his thinking; although one suspects nothing is lost thereby.

whatever sequence one chooses. I experienced them as a quartet, however, an ensemble that, taken together, tells a story. My preferred sequence begins with an introduction to Goethe, Steiner and the threefold image of society, in which Behrens says of Goethe, that "[he] himself did not succeed—and perhaps did not intend to—in grasping the central impulse of historic and social life in the same conceptual way he conceived and proved the reality of nature's ideas." Although I beg to differ on this point, Behrens nevertheless goes on to say that, "in the sense of Goethe's world conception and its development through anthroposophy, it is not possible to establish a truly practical social science if the observing and reporting of outer facts, and the theoretical formulation of their laws, are not supplemented by methodical observation and cognition of spiritual life."[34] In effect, Behrens continues, "the social sciences such as history, ethnography, psychology, political

---

34 I should advise the reader that, although this commentary was written unawares of what my colleagues were writing, it took place in between, as it were, two other studies I was engaged in at the same time. The first—*Shakespeare, Englishness and Finance*—concerned Shakespeare and his destiny as represented by Frederick Hiebel in *Shakespeare and the Awakening of Modern Consciousness* (Anthroposophic Press, New York, 1940), namely, as the key representative of what one might call Englishness, that quality that was to "lead the rest of the world in the development of the principle of the consciousness soul," something that in fact began in 1215 at the time of King John and Magna Carta, i.e., two centuries prior to the Renaissance. The second—*Goethe, Finance and the Gray Time*—was an immersion in *Goethe and Money*, the previously cited collection of essays that includes many surprising jewels of information, including that Goethe staged Shakespeare's play, *King John*, as his first theater production in 1791. But especially Goethe's maxim, so pertinent to Bernhard Behrens's own observations, that "the person acting is always without conscience; none has conscience but the person observing."

science, sociology and economics are nothing but variations of the 'science of freedom,' as Rudolf Steiner called them when expounding the fundamentals of Goethe's world conception." This establishes the mood for Behrens's social scientific enquiry with its particular use of methodical observation and cognition, the foundational result of which is that, "the individual human being, can only be considered as a threefold entity composed of body, soul and spirit [and that] as soon as man is recognized[35] as such an entity, the general form of the social organism and its laws will also be recognized."[36]

From here, in Behrens's treatment, one can identify and hopefully go on to establish "the conditions vital to [that threefold] social organism." He is forthright in his insights and advice: "...the social organism is given us not as a fruit, but as a task." Similarly, "...both good and evil have access to the boundless regions of liberty. The two sides of existence, the light and the dark, have acquired equal opportunity for action, and the human being has the choice of identifying himself with one or the other. Potential freedom is the signature of our time." And again, when he says the nations of the world (the essay quoted from was written seven years after the 1944 Bretton Woods conference) need to achieve a worldwide scope in order to see their missions in the light of each other—a view

---

35 *Shakespeare and the awakening of Modern Consciousness.* Frederick Hiebel, Anthroposophic Press, New York, 1940.

36 That said, there are moments when Behrens drops his social scientific stance, his frequent use of *only,* for example, giving to his argument at times an insistent tone.

very reminiscent of the "own light" and "choir of cultures" imagery I often draw attention to.[37]

If I have a query here it concerns Behrens's notion of "anthropocracy"! I am not sure if he means something positive by it. It sounds like the principle of democracy gone supra- if not super-national, when it should remain national. That democracy is universally experienced, or potentially so, I do not doubt, but in my understanding its implementation should stay national or country-based, even if the "same" form is used. International arbitration and cooperation do not require global governance, for example; both can be effected by harmonization.

On the other hand, in *Death and Life of Democracy*, Behrens's treatment of democracy as spirit-born is very powerful, as something we need first to value spiritually if we are to give it effect in the realm of governments, voting and elections. In his words, "[t]he democratic idea, which represents a profoundly moral intuition, can only be realized through moral imagination [something that] arising out of intuition, will be required in order to solve the problems of life in a practical way. The moral technique of action will [then] have a healing effect." Added to this, Behrens's distinction between personality and individuality is as impressive as it is informative, not to mention challenging! His various explications enable one to step back from today's chaotic interpretations of democracy—especially that fraudulent binary thing, "Western democracy"—and catch one's historical breath, the better to frame one's political comprehension and guide one's voting finger.

---

37 For example, in *Finance at the Threshold: Rethinking the Real and Financial Economies*, Christopher Houghton Budd, Gower, 2011.

≈

With the social sciences well-rooted, the conditions of three-fold social life recognized, and democracy "rebooted," the stage is set for Bernhard Behrens's treatment of economics, business and finance. *The Economic Essentials of Spiritual Life* is the longest of the four essays reviewed here and the one that suggests this is where my still unknown author has his habitat. Behrens covers a lot of ground here in a way that feels both informed and informative.

And yet, Behrens writes with a "free enterprise" bent, which put me on alert. In my experience of the business world in the United States, quite apart from its "frat" culture, its background lodges and masonry, and its untoward involvement in supremacist geopolitics (as if that were not enough), there is the ever-present moment when discourse on the economy slips into John Galt mode, when a certain cold spirit takes hold of things, as exemplified in Ayn Rand's life and work, for example, and well summed up in her newsletter's title, *The Objectivist*. Behrens presumably hints at such things when he refers to those "forces of impetus and of resistance [that] have driven social forms and conditions into chaos; and out of disintegrated matter and anarchistic forces...have contrived with superhuman lawlessness to construct a spiritless, sub-human domain fueled like a gigantic machine with the degraded will-substance of mankind," and when he warns of an "abyss of perdition [yawning] deeper and blacker." (If Behrens is not referring to this, it is not clear what he has in mind. On the other hand, eternal after death damnation, spiritual ruin, loss of soul are hefty images!)

In the United States, it is the Galtian spirit one has to contend with in all matters to do with associative economics—for it breathes a different air, inhabits different heights and would lead human history down quite different pathways to those Rudolf Steiner has in mind.

As far as I know, few speak or write in this way in threefold, world economy circles, and yet without this context modern understanding of economic life, and its related sciences, stands to be as chaotic as that concerning democracy. Somewhat diffidently, therefore, in presenting what struck me as its highlights, I would like nevertheless to challenge Behrens's version of things. I do so for the sake of research and scholarship, but also in a sense to commune with him *post mortem*—and others like him, such as Ralph Courtney. Such men belong to the initial efforts to convey Steiner's ideas into the world of "wasps" (white Anglo-Saxon protestants). Their endeavors (like similar ones at the time in Great Britain) may have disappeared into the sands or karsts of recent history but they need to be sought again and traced in their further possibilities.

In doing so, my main concern is that, at least to an English soul, it is all too easy to locate the driver of change in the outer aspect of rights life (i.e., laws), rather than its inner origin as a sense of right. All too often, when trying to enter into the spirit of associative economics, the role of the associative mind and non-egotistical conduct is leapfrogged or overlooked. The human being is critiqued for being selfish and exhorted not to remain so, especially in economic affairs, but then not credited with the ability actually to be or become altruistic. Rather than positing altruistic financial behavior and then describing what that might look like, prescriptive suggestions arise instead as to how an altruistic economy would or should work. In short, in much of the discussion concerning associative economics, its agency is seldom located in the user of capital (i.e., the entrepreneur) and his or her altruistic spirit, but remains with the owners and providers of it.

In Bernhard Behrens's case, this might have to do with how at times he falls into the trap of trying to describe the overall working of socioeconomic life, always a risky thing to do without sounding, as he does, occasionally patrician. That said, in his defense, what may come across as that is probably linked to the German or even Continental (but not characteristic of Great Britain or the United States) tradition of cameralism, what today might be called the benign state.

≈

My self-appointed task takes up space that some may regard as disproportionate,[38] but to my mind there is no point in not interrogating what Bernhard Behrens has written. Others can challenge me back; but there is too much at stake to leave such discussions light and polite. Europeans often hold the United States askance, and yet it is there, arguably, that Steiner's counsel needs to be heeded most. This will not happen if, conversely, one has no expectation of innate right economic action already there—latent, for sure, but perhaps already running in channels hidden by our preconceptions. With the aim of using a methodical and cognitive approach matching Behrens's own, I will proceed by way of examples

---

38   I did not anticipate my colleagues' contributions would be so short!

of what I mean. As stand-alone statements, his observations all sound innocent enough, but I am left uneasy by them.

Always in the background is the idea of spiritual life distinct from economic life and that those in (or claiming to be in) the former have some kind of superiority. Insofar as a coin has two sides, however, and inasmuch as Steiner makes clear that spiritual life and economic life are related as a nut to its shell,[39] this can never be. The human I is not identified with and does not reside in only one of society's domains, namely, spiritual life. It inhabits all three, just as one's I is not found only in one's thinking or metabolism, but in all three of the soul's dimensions. Get that wrong, and John Galt soon makes his appearance.

Behrens makes substantial reference to sacrifice, even suggesting—or so it seems to me—that congregations sacrifice for the sake of their priests. But is that ever really so? In my experience of them, most priests receive a "living" independently of their congregations. Moreover, its true source can often be elsewhere, including property sales and financial market earnings. Referencing Bernhard Laum,[40] what would Behrens make of Gerard Klockenbring's idea, for example, that sacrifice concerns what we give away out of

---

39 "…the economic life of a particular time, and the spiritual life of a particular time (the times are not quite identical), hold the same relation as a nut to its shell; the economic life is invariably the shell which the spiritual life has thrown out. It takes its cast from the spiritual life. Today's abstract economic life is, therefore, the product of an abstract spiritual life. That is why today we are in an age of abstract thinking, of life-remoteness—unreal conjunctures and such things" ("The Abstract Nature of Modern Economic Life," in Rudolf Steiner and Christopher Houghton Budd, *Rudolf Steiner, Economist: Articles and Essays*. New Economy Publications, Canterbury 2018 [1996]).

40 Bernhard Laum, *Das Heilige Geld*, Tübingen, 1924.

our excess, not our necessities?[41] Absent such a notion, what does the statement, that "surplus [derives] from individual willingness to make sacrifices" imply other than a latter-day Protestant work ethic?

One of the rawest of nerves is touched by Bernhard Behrens's remarking that "the rights life will protect the disposal of capital, or means of production, and real estate, as long as such property is administered in the general interest." Here, precisely, the question arises whether we really do need some kind of trust arrangements (like land trusts, or the Purpose

---

41 As far back as our knowledge takes us we know that human beings made sacrifices. These sacrifices entailed offering something from one's environment that was necessary for one's spiritual life but not for one's livelihood. In this way, a vacuum or emptiness was created, which gave rise to new forces. Certain human beings—those with insight into mystery-filled higher laws—could make these forces accessible to their fellows by receiving and making sacrifices. The sacrifices belonged to the gods as an expression of the spiritual— that is to say, of thoughts, of a dialogue with the gods. In the course of time, this attitude towards sacrifice brought about a growth of human consciousness, and intercourse with the higher powers became increasingly characterized by mutual understanding. "In Greece the relationship between God and man was one of free exchange. The same applied to other historical religions." In Gerard Klockenbring, *History of Money,* New Economy Publications, Canterbury, England, 2004 [1974].

CHB: Surplus does not arrive from a "willingness to make sacrifices." It arises because, as spiritual beings on earth, we cannot help but create wealth in excess of our earthly needs, wealth that has to flow away from us. It did so very evidently when the Vikings flooded out of Northern Europe, carried by their excess will forces. The only sacrifices then were on the part of those they descended upon. If Marx and the capitalists he critiqued had understood this, we would never have suffered the deep calamity of today's perennial struggle over the ownership, rather than *use*, of surplus value. Accounting shows that profits flow away from the trading accounts onto the balance sheet, just as reserves flow away into banks. Gift money, understood economically, allows this flow away to continue. This will never be experienced in its economic rawness if we begin with the moralism implicit in Behrens's treatment of sacrifice. Surplus is simply consequent on man being man.

Foundation in Germany, or B Corps) or whether people need to be trusted (albeit also educated to do so) to "extirpate their own egoism root and branch" directly in their own economic lives by using their assets and circumstances consciously as vehicles and vessels, even chalices, for the will forces and unfolding destinies of others than themselves? And not only others in their own blood line. I admit to being hyperallergic in this regard, but for me there is a world of difference between the state reflecting and facilitating altruistic behavior on my part, and requiring it of me, let alone the idea that it can cause such conduct.

I understand well enough—indeed, it is somewhat stating the obvious—that in any healthy enterprise some capital of its own generation is ploughed back in immediately, while another part of it is retained for "a rainy day," and that substantial amounts can also be held in reserve that are in fact lent out via the financial system to other enterprises in the rest of the world. I understand, too, that some, at least, of this excess can (and even should) be transferred to schools and cultural institutions such as opera houses and the like, as revenue—to be spent on teachers' and singers' salaries—but not as capital for investing in premises. This already, and readily, happens today where egotism is *not* the watchword. Indeed, how else is egotism to be transformed? And what anyway underpins simple normal giving?

If this is what Bernhard Behrens has in mind when he says,

> Capital diverted into the spiritual sphere is completely consumed and must be continually replaced by new donations from the economy. It must not flow back into the economy, i.e., the gift-money has to be withdrawn from circulation by the banking organization

in accordance with the date of expiration. Invested money, on the contrary, does return to the economy where it serves to establish, perfect, or extend economic enterprises,

all well and good, but I remain unconvinced by such structural conceptions. It is but one step from there to go on to say that capital is nowadays only managed by executives who no longer work with capital belonging to them, but with capital that others have placed at their disposal. This may be true as a generality in corporate finance,[42] but there are many cases where individuals remain linked directly to their capital, albeit via fiduciary agents. And, of course, most corporate capital is owned by millions of individual human beings, again admittedly via managed agglomerations such as pensions funds.[43]

More to the point, this is still about the use of capital at the behest of its owners rather than its users. And it is still about capital under the sign of preservation, not circulation—the latter two being, to my mind, important and central leitmotifs of associative economics. Finally, capital is managed today precisely because shareholders see managers as their servants in the business of profit creation, and not as entrepreneurs to whose wings they wish to give lift, so that, together with them, they can fulfill purposes higher than quarter-day profit distributions, irrespective of what

---

42 In fact, however, it is not the case when they have substantial stock holdings in the companies they run.

43 While the criticism is possibly historically premature, as regards the times Behrens lived in, if one really wants to act with associative monetary awareness today, one can do so using one's own accounting system and direct lending possibilities rather than those of third parties.

they "make" their money in or from, and without regard to how they make it.

If this critique seems hard on Behrens, it is only because he is not here to defend his statements in person. Even so, they need to be challenged, especially if in publishing them now they are thought thereby to be endorsed wholesale, rather than seen as the opportunity they afford—even at this late date—to open up much-needed debate. (Imagine if this debate had happened 75 years ago, the more so if it had been able to break ground!)

Here are two more sentiments that make me ill at ease:

> …only the bearers of spiritual life, called to such office by virtue of character, knowledge and experience, can judge which personalities are morally and practically equipped to handle loaned capital for productive purposes. Summing up: the spiritual sphere would not function economically—that is, it would replace neither the promoter, the manager nor the bank; but it would act in an advisory capacity with legal status in matters of directing and investing capital. In this sense only would the administration of capital become a task of the spiritual sphere.

> The reason why such a valid opinion can be formed in the free realm of culture is because there alone exists the requisite independence from egotistical special interests, one-sided, collectivistic ideas on economic planning, political considerations, and the influence of pressure groups.

As to the first, how can an advisor have powers of direction? Second, why are entrepreneurs thought *not* to be in the "spiritual realm"? In following out one's destiny, who is *not* heeding or fulfilling a calling, a vocation? The entrepreneur is as much in the spiritual life as the teacher, as Rudolf Steiner himself makes clear in the preface to the 1920 edition of *The Threefold Nature of Social Life*.

Concerns such as these, both conceptually formulated and based on years of experience, lead me to be on guard, lest what Behrens benignly intends becomes translated in practice into the tyranny of trustees and those who have never "made money," and so arguably have no real entrepreneurial knowledge of money, nor of the opportunity direct use of capital *on one's own responsibility* provides to experience and practice non-egotism.

> Upon this confidence rests the sort of credit indispensable to modern economy.

> There purchase money combines with individual ability, which is also a consequence of man's relation to spiritual life; and the degree to which individual ability has risen through schooling, self-education and experience determines the social form of production and its capacity for covering general needs. Such ability includes not only expert knowledge and technical skill, but moral qualities as well.

Again, such statements unnerve me because of their seeming innocence. While true enough on the surface, they give rise in me to the feeling I have when I hear a capitalist talking to workers, whose labor he thinks he is buying; not an entrepreneur among fellow entrepreneurs—they making the parts of a car, he putting it together and finding a buyer for it. Let alone the world of sole proprietors and self-employed. Misread or misapplied, these remarks come dangerously close to an external authority knowing what is best for one; where what is moral is external to one and exercised through money.[44] I would think differently if, underscoring the moral element, Behrens had pointed to karma and an individual's past life development, let alone future tasks. But he did not do so; nor to how capitalizing initiative can awaken such things and give them agency. That said, in the essay on *Goethe and the Social Question*, Behrens does refer to Goethe's view that the "essence of capital cannot be recognized by notions which merely refer to an amount of money, a collection of means of production, or to an interest-bearing investment."

Finally, albeit at risk of being naïve, there is also that subtlest of concerns: namely, that the challenge of positivism[45] will not be met out of moral injunctions. It has, as it were, to be allowed its expression, not only so that the error of its way may be experienced *post facto* (and other than theoretically), but by those, moreover, who then become its erstwhile proponents. Our experience of morality *within* economic and financial dealings has to be born again, but cannot do so if one continues to experience capital as something coming to one from without rather than within.[46]

In all this, I may, of course, be seeing ghosts that do not exist. For what is to be doubted when Behrens writes:

> We believe we have shown that even the purely scientific concept "purchase money," with its relation to the concepts "loan money" and "gift money," throws light upon the true relation of economic to spiritual life, arousing the will to an ever more conscious shaping

---

44 Immediately after the Second World War, of course, it was the norm for many ordinary people that their economies, their income and their mortgages were controlled by their employers.

45 See footnote 68.

46 A possibility implicit in any "true" non-monetary conception of capital and alluded to, ironically, by Behrens himself in footnote 65 and the passage to which that footnote belongs.

of this relation. In practice, such a conscious shaping would work out as a voluntary limiting of individual needs in order to reduce extravagance and the manufacture of goods that are economically and culturally superfluous.

Yes, sort of, until one asks who is to define extravagance and superfluity? And why not, instead, aver the Aristotelian notion of "enoughness"? I also remain ever wary of the notion that loans and loan money are synonyms or equivalents, and bridle at the like idea concerning gifts and gift money.

> The money and labor thereby saved could be made available for the spiritual life in ever greater measure. This is the method by which, within the total social organism, the independent economic foundation could be laid for bringing forth great creations, notably monumental works of art, through spiritual activity... Unscrupulous economic exploitation of nature and the senseless waste of products manufactured out of her raw materials and forces would be replaced by careful cultivation and transformation—a testimony to the awakening of the human spirit. The more thrifty economy is on the consumption side, the more lavishly can spiritual life unfold when munificence, in the creative sense, is in order.

Again, what is my complaint here? Not only that the spirit comes of itself, not at the behest of ornamenting a townscape, but also the very image of spiritual life being synonymous with munificence, however meant, when, in my mind spiritual life should refer to the capitalization of every single human being's initiative—including that of the monumental artist.

Finally, when Behrens says that, "[the state] will leave the organization and circulation of money to an associatively constituted (better put, conducted?) economy, limiting its own function to the guaranteeing of the legal status of money as a public medium of exchange," I wonder what his take was on modern monetary science. In Steiner's economics course, there is no place or need for central banks, which are mutually exclusive to associative economic conduct. In monetary history generally, especially recently, this is known well enough, but it is caught on the divide between those on the "left" who, knowing that thereby they gain great power, seek to maintain central banks but as state agents. And those on the "right" who, seeking to wrest this power away from governments, advocate central banks becoming subservient to financial markets.

What especially, it would be interesting to know, did Bernhard Behrens make of the US Federal Reserve System, money creation, and the many issues that are alive in today's monetary reform movement, with which not a few "three-folders" identify? And what was his view of the "Austrian" economists? For example, Hayek's argument[47] that no issuer of money, least of all the state, should be able to claim exclusive legal tender status for its money, that free acceptance is the decider of all issue. Or of Keynes's 1923 *Tract on Monetary Reform*,[48] which seeks to displace centralized monetary conduct with "deliberate and scientific" behavior on the part of everyone? Both these arguments were matters of high debate at the time Behrens was writing.

---

47 In *The Denationalisation of Money.* Hobart Paper 70, IEA, FA Hayek, October 1976.

48 J. M. Keynes, *A Tract on Monetary Reform,* Macmillan, London, 1923.

I focus on this for two reasons. Firstly, denying the state's money legal tender status delinks the state from economic life in one fell swoop of the ax—such a separation of state and economy being one of the hallmarks of a threefold social order. Secondly, for reasons there is not time now to introduce, it compels one to understand not only Steiner's idea of three kinds of money, which Behrens speaks of substantially, but their "operationalizing" via Steiner's related idea of a one-world currency based on "money as bookkeeping," about which, however, Behrens is wholly and therefore strangely silent.

≈

I do not want to end this assessment on a churlish note, however, or give the impression that I am not attentive to deeper aspects of Bernhard Behrens's interest or respectful of his endeavors. The problem is that I am not aware of anything he has written that I would describe as of a Rosicrucian nature,[49] though he may well have done so outside the essays under consideration here. Plus, he is no longer here to ask—other than through the medium of these contemplations.

So, I will end on a Rosicrucian note of my own devising. To Behrens's statement, that

> [modern techniques provide] the external conditions under which the individual can enjoy economic

---

49 By Rosicrucian, I mean, for example, that one should beware thinking the bone is solid, an obstacle that one has to go around, as it were; that the physical world is non-permeable and not permeated by the non-physical. Indeed, close-up a human bone is a honeycomb of interconnected holes. We need to be careful not to focus on the material at the expense of the porous. Similarly, fixity frames flexibility and is not estranged from or inimical to it.

independence; and the latter can have social meaning only through the attainment and realization of inner freedom in the realm of spiritual activity. This realization manifests itself socially as a widening and deepening of the knowledge of man and the cosmos, of the manifestation of truth through art, and of the perfecting of the imperfect through religion...

I would add that the same is true when a person finds and is able to fulfill his or her destiny or reason for being on earth *through the very way he or she is brought to financial literacy* and *through the very way his or her unfolding destiny is financed*.

To reach such an experience, however, deep thought needs to be given to passing references in Behrens's anthology that it would be well for everyone, whether anthroposophist, Anglo-Saxon, Goetheanist or Shakespearian, to ponder. For each has much to learn from the other. For example, the increase of habitable land, whether by swamp draining or dyking the sea is not, as such, an object, cause or creature of land speculation, as is sometimes the assumed moral of the story of Goethe's *Faust*. The Lowlands, for example, and all who live in them, owe their existence to much invention in this field.

When Goethe looked "beyond the seas" to that place now known as the United States,[50] was he thinking physically and politically, or was he being mindful of the fledgling nature of the United States' constitutional and financial history—to wit, for example, what do its citizens understand by the expression, "We, the people..."? Or was he thinking metaphysically—of the strange fraternity

---

50   In fact, Templar and other histories include the eastern coast of today's Canada.

of Bacon and Shakespeare and of how Isaac Newton and John Locke may have been party to it? Not entirely slave to Baconian thinking but under its primary influence, such that their non-Baconian thoughts can only be found peeping out between the lines of what they wrote and lived. But extant nonetheless. I say this lest anthroposophical epithets cast about on Rudolf Steiner's say-so lead us past, or to overlook, what may prove to be an unexplored dimension in the biographies and work of both men, as well as others whose destinies might be similarly freighted.

5

Commentary on Behrens's Essays

Stephen Vallus

[In the form of natural science], the worldviews that are founded on a more religious basis...accept the traditions that have been handed down without penetrating to their fountainhead in the depths of human nature. [In addition,] spiritual science...develops epistemological methods that lead down into those regions of our inner nature where the processes external to us find their continuation within human nature itself.... These insights shape themselves into ideas that are not mere mental constructs, but rather something saturated with the forces of reality. Hence...they [can] offer themselves as guides to social action.[51]

Bernhard Behrens began publishing in the United States in 1944 after emigrating here from Germany during the Second World War. Imbued with Rudolf Steiner's work in economics and sociology, his essays still resonate in the present time. With the relief that came with the war's end, he can perhaps be forgiven for being too optimistic regarding the prospects of the victorious United States in taking up its new

---

51 Rudolf Steiner, "Culture, Law, and Economics," in *The Renewal of the Social Organism,* Steinerbooks, 1985 (CW 24).

role in world history. To wit: "It is precisely through a fully conscious grasp of the idealistic human forces in America, reaching out beyond national frontiers, that the democratic ideal can be carried toward its ever-purer realization."

One wishes he would have examined Keynes's (and Great Britain's) proposal of the *bancor* at the 1944 Bretton Woods Conference. From the French *banque or* ("bank gold"), this functioning unit of account would have replaced the gold standard (not to mention eventual US dollar hegemony) in the postwar financial order. Of course, the United States insisted on its "top-dog" status rather than Keynes's essentially cooperative arrangement. Of particular interest in the *bancor's* design is the fact that (trade) surpluses by member countries would be subject to fines, thereby discouraging the accruing or privatizing of gains by creditor countries to the detriment of debtors.

One theme that emerges in these essays is that of forbearance in the face of power. Notwithstanding its Keynesian pedigree, different to the "enforced" restraint of the *bancor*, we have the Swiss cultural theorist, Denis de Rougemont,[52] who was concerned with the political reorganization of Europe after the Second World War. He was also speaking in the same period of history as Behrens, who refers to the democratic life of Switzerland in Kahler's work *Man the Measure* (1943).[53] After six years of exile in the United States, de Rougemont returned to Switzerland to give a historic speech in Montreux in 1947 at the meeting of the Union of European Federalists. In there, his first

---

52 Denis de Rougemont, *L'attitude fédéraliste* (The federalist attitude), L'Aubier, Neuchâtel, Switzerland, 2012.

53 Erich Kahler, *Man the Measure: A New Approach to History*, George Braziller, New York, 1956.

"principle of federalism" refers to the renunciation of hegemony between Catholics and Protestants, which resulted in the Swiss Constitution of 1848. In the dynamic thinking of de Rougemont, man in society is pictured as both "*free and responsible,* both autonomous and united." This complements Behrens's description, after Goethe, of "the archetype of Man, [in whom the] two manifestations of human existence (thinking and willing) are united."

But as Behrens warns us: "Until true individualism—meaning not the continuation but the overcoming of egoism—has the strength to win through against and transform the artificially galvanized group spirits [from the past], the task of culture cannot be fulfilled. Group interests will continue to act as mutual enemies."

This battle will not be won either on the town square or in the halls of Congress, but rather, I would aver, in our personal unfolding of economic life, which by its very nature is done in concert with others. While the practicalities associated with this assertion are beyond the scope of these essays, all students of economics and sociology (not just specialists!) would do well to live with the story told in these short tracts.

6

Goethe and the Social Question

Goethe's life belonged to a time of far-reaching social changes. The transformation of consciousness that occurred at and after the end of the Middle Ages produced immense effects within the social life of the 18th and 19th centuries. In consequence of this transformation of consciousness, the Europeans—and at the same time the "American" settlers—changed their relation to thought, nature, and the social order. The world of ideas was no longer experienced as an objective spiritual reality to which human reason can have access. During the Middle Ages, the representatives of Platonic and Aristotelian realism still had this experience. But now an idea was considered as a merely subjective and formal product of the human soul in the sense of medieval nominalism.

Since Francis Bacon (1561–1626), thinking turned away from the spiritual realities of ideas and attached itself more and more to the phenomena of outer nature. From that time on, sense perceptions were evaluated as the only constituents of a reality worthy of scientific inquiry. Logical thinking, especially in its mathematical form, became the tool of an expedient registration and classification of natural facts and of an abstract formulation of the laws that govern physical nature.

This kind of thinking was interested only in the calculable, that is, quantitative, part of nature, which can be perceived by the senses. The essence of the incalculable (qualitative) side of sense phenomena was more or less neglected. And the opinion spread, that this latter does not belong to reality at all. The qualitative part of the experienced world was looked on as the mere result of the soul's subjective reaction to the measurable influences acting upon her from the outer world according to causal law.

The conviction grew that an idea also can be nothing but a subjective outgrowth of consciousness. Thought was no longer experienced in its objective quality revealed through nature, as it was perceived during the times of Hellenistic philosophy:

> Thus, the creations of self-consciousness and of the observations of natural phenomena confront each other with increasing detachment, as if separated by an abyss. Through Descartes (1596–1650) that change of soul life which separates the image of nature from the creations of self-consciousness proclaims itself.[54]

Newton's friend, the philosopher John Locke (1632-1704), who originally was a physician, advanced this intellectual movement in a decisive way, while Newton himself was striving to develop an authoritative exposition of it in physics and astronomy. David Hume (1711–1776) and Immanuel Kant (1724–1804), both contemporaries of Goethe, brought this trend of thought and science to a climax by establishing the dogma of the unalterable limitations of human knowledge. Kant's dogma, that "I had to discard knowledge in

---

54 Rudolf Steiner, *The Riddles of Philosophy*. Anthroposophic Press, New York, 1973.

order to make room for faith," seemed so indisputable that it became generally accepted, with fateful consequences.

The separation of faith from knowledge was accomplished. Culture, in the sense of a religion, art, and science, ceased to be a matter of general interest. It became a more or less private affair and the servant of a questionable cultivation of personality within exclusive circles. Public life became more and more accustomed to and satisfied with "civilization" as the dubious substitute for true culture. The powerfully unfolding science of outer nature, with its utilitarian application, became the main subject of public interest. Thus, this science became the source of that 18th and 19th century onrush of civilization through the Industrial Revolution, which, in the name of "progress" swept away the remnants of time-honored cultural values.

Goethe watched the Industrial Revolution with intense interest. The scope of his interests included everything; he was a true cosmopolitan. The decisive invention of the steam engine (Watt, 1769), the inventions of spinning and weaving machines (Hargreaves, 1767; Arkwright, Crompton, 1779), and all the other important steps in the establishment of the English textile industry, belong to Goethe's time. He watched how, first in England, the iron and coal industry were put on their modem foundations, and how the mass production of tools and of pottery was established.

Goethe was a witness of the way in which the economic life of the European West became enmeshed in the development of the factory system. And he saw how the latter, by means of the construction of canals, bridges and harbors, forced the acceleration of the technical development of the transportation system. To Goethe's lifetime belongs the opening of the first railroad, which since 1830 connected Manchester with Liverpool. He felt delight over the use for the first time of the balloon (1783) as a means of travel, but was less enthusiastic about the implications inherent in the changes introduced into the business and banking systems in line with modern ideas.[55]

The fast and powerful growth of capitalism and the rapid emergence of all its essential features could be watched by Goethe. He was also able to note the way the social question[56] had already made itself felt in those times. They were the times when, in France, social reformers like Saint Simon and Fourier were at work. Because their ideas were supposed to appeal to human reason and the heart, their successors, who started to preach the doctrine of class struggle, called them "Utopists." It was these Utopists who coined the terms "socialism" and "individualism" and introduced them as conceptual tools for the unfolding of the materialistic social sciences, and as aids in the discussion of sociological and economic problems.

The change of the political world situation that Goethe had to face reflected the transformation of consciousness even more strikingly than did the Industrial Revolution. Politically, Germany was nothing more than a conglomerate of many individual states of different size and power, most of them governed by absolutist monarchs. These states lived in the shadow of a traditional but powerless empire that was on its way out. In France, in consequence of the Revolution, the old ruling powers were replaced by the bourgeoisie. This produced the conditions for the transitory but influential

---

55 For a detailed account of Goethe in this respect, see *Goethe and Money*. op. cit.

56 I.e., the relation between capital and labor. —Ed.

phenomenon of Napoleon Bonaparte's empire, an attempt to unify Europe by military force.

All this happened one hundred years after England had brought her own (Glorious) Revolution to a successful end (1688), thus paving the way for the development of parliamentarianism (and constitutional monarchy). This form of government offered the intellectual and political background not only to the Industrial Revolution and the change of all habits of life, but also to the rise of the fourth estate, the proletariat.[57]

The social question, as we experience it today in its distressing impact and worldwide scope, was born during Goethe's lifetime under the auspices of Western parliamentarianism. It was but a short time after Goethe's death (1832) that Karl Marx and Friedrich Engels wrote their *Communist Manifesto* (1848), after they had investigated the position of the proletariat, especially the English factory workers. Later on, in England, Karl Marx wrote *Das Kapital.*

To the Goethean period belongs the aftermath of the Peace of Nystadt (1721), in consequence of which Russia, as a new Great Power, entered the Council of Nations. Prior to this, Peter the Great had opened Russia's gates to the influx of Western civilization. Almost at the same time, the United

---

57 CHB: As explored in my essay, *Goethe, Finance and the Gray Time* (unpublished), Behrens's description of the fourth estate as the proletariat is at odds with both Goethe and the latent tricameral parliament in England, comprising the three political parties that represent land (Conservatives), capital (Liberals) and labor (Labour). Interestingly, often when the pregnancy of threefoldness in social life appears, but is not recognized, a fourth, false, aspect is invented, like the so-called fourth function of money (deferred payment). Or the Fourth King in Goethe's fairy tale. But, like the Mixed King, this has to collapse: it is the faux expression of the I, due to its mixing up rather than interweaving the three aspects of society.

States was on the verge of finishing her period of colonial dependence. After the Peace of Paris (1763) and their successful War of Independence, the United States of America, as the first country with representative government and also (1787) a written Constitution,[58] was prepared to cast a decisive word into the scales of world affairs. It is significant that the fateful world-antagonism of Russian absolutism to the United States' democratic way of life can be traced back to Goethe's time.

Not only did Goethe look with interest at the central events of his time—the French Revolution and Napoleon's fall—but he observed with concern also the growing nationalistic forces at work in his own country. Narrow-minded nationalism was not to his cosmopolitan taste. He affirmed his position toward the ideas of the French Revolution in such literary works as *Conversations of German Emigrants, Hermann and Dorothea,* and *The Natural Daughter.*

What Goethe wanted is intelligently expressed in the preface to a new edition of *Conversations of German Emigrants*: "It was to defend and protect the endangered cultivation of human harmony. This he did in the midst of questionable political struggle and strife, and in the presence of disintegration in all hitherto undisputed forms of life."[59]

In spite of the rise of Prussia, the Germany of Goethe's time was not a decisive political power, and even less a weighty economic one. But Germany gave birth to the spiritual-cultural light of German idealism. The heartening

---

58 CHB: Here is not the place to enter into the subject, but one needs to tread carefully; before the Constitution was adopted, there were the Articles of Confederation.

59 J. W. Goethe, *Conversations of German Emigrants,* Maria Honeit, Hamburg.

struggle of this idealism for spiritual freedom, artistic creation of eternal human values, and philosophical rebirth of religious life upon a higher level of consciousness, has found its towering representative in Goethe.

The spiritual-cultural impulse that lived in Goethe was not only a source of inspiration to his genius as an artist, it manifested itself also in his indefatigable Faustian struggle for truth and in his painstaking and persistent scientific research. To Goethe, the thorny path of knowledge was identical with the road leading to freedom. Freedom was to him the light-pervaded spiritual atmosphere in which his works in many fields were born. Thus, Goethe represented the very heart of the spiritual organism of German idealism that, in its turn was the cosmopolitan center of all true cultural endeavors in those times. The educated world loved this idealism, and with disgust turned away from Germany one hundred years after Goethe's death, when (1933), under the ill-advised dictatorship of political and economic expediency, she forsook her spiritual mission by failing to fulfill the directives of Goethe's testament.

Only those who can perceive the creative light of spiritual freedom in Goethe's work and personality are able to value this work as the incorruptible seed of a true cosmopolitan culture. The fructifying of this seed would if it were permitted to, work with a clarifying and ordering force within the present social chaos, and it would provide a vitalizing power never dreamt of. Goethe did not contribute anything to the solution of the social question in scientific works of a sociological, political or economic pattern like those of philosophers such as Adam Smith, John Locke, David Hume, John Stuart Mill, Auguste Comte and

Herbert Spencer. The aim of these philosophers was to grasp the "objective" laws of the social structure and thus enable the human being to adjust himself and his activities to such laws. Goethe's ideal was to conceive the true spiritual intentions and activities at work within nature and man. He wanted to make his fellow men aware of man's destiny: To be himself the creator of the social organism and to endow it with order and lawfulness.

Goethe's contributions to the solution of the social question are his artistic work as a whole, as well as his striving to cope with the problems of natural science.[60] A response on our part in keeping with this work would bring about a transformation in our materialistic way of thinking and habits of life—a transformation that would bring people to a true world conception and a social order for which our time is longing.

This character of Goethe's work becomes even more transparent in the light of the fact that Goethe the scientist and research worker "did not," as Rudolf Steiner expressed it, "follow any personal inclination, but the kind of art he was devoted to aroused inner needs that could be satisfied only through scientific activity." Both trends have their wellspring in a profound religious impulse. "They meet at a point where accomplishment in respect of one domain asks for accomplishment in respect of the other."

---

60   CHB: The many scholarly essays in the previously cited *Goethe and Money* show this is not the case. Strangely, Behrens seems to miss his own point—namely, that not only were many of Goethe's literary works social commentary, but such observations as the role of bookkeeping (no less!) as a guide in life in *Wilhelm Meister*, for example and mentioned himself, were born of concrete entrepreneurial and political experience on Goethe's part.

Goethe expressed this through the words: "He who has science and art has religion also. He who does not have them should have religion."

The basic social impulse in Goethe's work comes most impressively to light through his great novel *Wilhelm Meister*. The hero is presented as a man guided by his destiny through a great variety of general human relationships and the life of distinguished circles with which he comes into intimate contact. These experiences provide him with the opportunity of developing his character and of gathering wisdom. Wilhelm starts as an apprentice, and proceeds as a journeyman of social life and acquires skill, experience and personal culture. At last he obtains the mature wisdom and moral strength that enable him to be a master of social life.

Wilhelm Meister travels the road of initiation. Two of his most illuminating experiences are brought about by his coming in contact respectively with a personality and a community. The personality is *Makarie*. She is a pure and unique being of highest morality and intelligence. She is blessed with a divine gift by which she is enabled—through some sort of clairvoyance of a mathematical exactitude[61]—to experience within her own soul the spirituality of the whole cosmic system, of the celestial bodies belonging to the sphere of the sun. Our solar system, with its inner meaning, is open to her spiritual perception. Her awe-inspiring presence influences her social surroundings in a most positive way. Thus, Makarie acts like a focus of spirit-born moral forces. The community is to be found in the chapter entitled *The Pedagogical Province*, which forms the highlight of the novel. This community embraces the living and working together of teachers and

---

61   An expression reminiscent of Steiner's description of arithmetic as the last vestige of ancient clairvoyance.

students in an ideal educational institution. By means of an inspired and methodical application of science, art and religion, the pupils give promise of becoming outstanding examples of true manhood. The ideal underlying this method of education is to be achieved by harmony of spirit, soul and body—that is, of truth, beauty and virtue.

The incorruptible foundation stone is laid by teaching, first, three kinds of awe-inspired devotion (*Ehrfurcht*): devotion to the spirituality of the universe that hovers above man, devotion to social life that unfolds around man, and devotion to earthly nature that is below man and carries his earthly weight during his earthly life. This attitude of devotion to the realm below includes also the pious acknowledgment of "baseness and pauperism, mockery and despicableness, disgrace and misery, suffering and death"—in short, the mysterious destiny of evil within the divine design of the world. One has the feeling of approaching the profoundest depths of Goethe's soul in its communion with the exalted idea of the transforming of evil into the good.

In the sense of Goethe, education means a social service by means of which our individual aptitudes and slumbering faculties are developed in such a way that everyone becomes prepared to put himself in the right place within society—and within the universe as well. The social consciousness itself becomes universal. The spiritual world permeates man, and, by his conscious mediation, human society also, with its divine forces. And the spiritual world receives them back again in the form of eternal human values. Goethe said, in *Faust*: "The trace of my earthly days cannot perish in eons." As the visitor is told by one of the three superiors of *The Pedagogical Province*: "We have to form the concept of a worldwide piety and to extend our honest aims, in a practical way, toward all, not only by helping our neighbors, but rather, by carrying along the whole of mankind at the same time."

Through every part of his comprehensive life work, Goethe shows that such a worldwide piety can be founded neither upon the dogma of blind faith nor upon the doctrines of an arrogantly theorizing philosophy. He knows that the innermost union with the world can grow only from awe-inspired devotion to that spirituality that reveals itself within man when he acquires a true knowledge of nature, experiences high art, and overcomes his egoism.

Goethe himself pointed to the basic social impulse inherent in his works. Thirty-two years after he had laid aside his unfinished poem, *The Mysteries (Die Geheimnisse)*, he was asked about its true meaning. Many years previously he had confessed, with the intellectual modesty that is so often the mark of great genius, that "this undertaking is too great for a man in my situation." Now, when he was asked the above question he characterized the social idea underlying this fragment, which tells of twelve elderly knights (all bearing in themselves a profound life experience) gathered around a thirteenth, named *Humanus*. The poet described how they form an exalted community in the spirit, "*Something like an ideal Montsalvat.*"

The twelve are to be considered representatives of various countries, world conceptions and religions. Each of them embodies some particular characteristic of the thirteenth. Each of them recognizes himself in this leader, and all feel themselves united with him, and thus with one another, upon a higher level of existence. This occurs in such a way that the fullness of the whole lives also in each individual knight. Thus, a universal community of human beings is established through the spirit. It is a community within which all that is individually characteristic does not perish but, rather, bears the whole and is borne by it. Indeed, a more impressive suggestion cannot be imagined for solving—on a spiritual-cultural foundation—the cardinal problem of bridging the abyss existing between individual men and society. The feeling that this is true is deepened by the fact that Goethe had originally planned to go on with the poem and to show how—among the knights—a newcomer of highest morality fulfills his destiny by taking over the exalted office of the leader. Having accomplished his mission, he is allowed to depart; taking leave with calm resolution, knowing that his spirit will live forever in the souls of the brethren.

Thus, Goethe had the intention of hinting at the dawn of a new age in which a new social order would be born through the rejuvenation of the dying spirituality of the cultures; this to come about on a new spiritual level in accordance with the demands of our time.

The same general impulse can be found at the foundation of all Goethe's artistic works. In the simplest way, it is expressed by that magnificent poem that begins with the words: "*Let man be noble, helpful and good, since that alone distinguishes him from all other beings…*"

It is more difficult to recognize Goethe's unique contributions to the solution of the social question in his scientific works and to evaluate rightly his *Aphorisms (Sprueche in Prosa),* which supplement them. We should be fully aware of the healthy influence that Goethe's scientific ideas and attainments could have upon the present crucial relation of the sciences to social life, were their significance recognized without prejudice; especially his method of acquiring knowledge, even more than the outer results of his research.

Goethe's nature had the capacity for discovering through scientific investigation, leading to living ideas, the hidden intentions of nature. A decisive, and frequently quoted, conversation with Schiller made Goethe aware of his genuine relationship to the world of ideas. He then became conscious of the fact that ideas were not, as claimed by the philosopher Kant, mere abstract regulative forms that emerge from the depths of the human organism in a subjective way and, therefore, cannot have any objective value for knowledge. To Goethe, ideas were not just useful mental forms for contemplating the unknowable, or for the mere classifying of sense phenomena. He did not consider them as mere convenient vehicles for the gathering of limited knowledge.

To Goethe, ideas were themselves the objects of knowledge, and the revelation of eternal truth, acquired through a spiritual activity that is limitless. Goethe saw ideas with the inner eye of the spirit. To him, they were "things in themselves"; that is, the creative forces of nature and of history. Through his perceptive power of thought (*anschauende Urteilskraft*), Goethe realized how a universal archetypal *idea*, that is to say, nature's intention proper, struggles to come to light through the metamorphosis of existence. This is a transformation that starts with the mineral kingdom, universally controlled by a macrocosmic law, proceeds from there toward the organic form of the plant, on to the ensouled animal organism, to be finally crowned by the human microcosm. In this latter, lives the archetypal idea of the universal whole. Goethe felt that the supreme World Spirit, by revealing Himself in the form of an idea, takes up His abode in the Holy of Holies of His temple built by Him through nature's powerful artistry over eons.

Man accomplishes something that nature cannot accomplish without him: the human being becomes nature's supreme organ for the perfection of her own wisdom, and hence carries out her intentions with love. Such intentions carried out in unselfish love are man's own moral intuitions. Through the actions of a self-conscious but unselfish personality, the spirit working through nature manifests itself within the body social that thus grows into a temple of all mankind.

The "greatest bliss of earthly children is nothing but personality!" exclaims Goethe. He knows that the Idea as the Word (Logos) of the eternal Spirit, when recognized in transitory phenomena, reveals the secret of nature's evolution: the development of mankind within the womb of the divine. But he knows also that during the evolution of history the divine manifests itself through man, who, as a free personality, acquires an understanding of his own nature with which his own idea is in conformity. It was Goethe's inner struggle to conceive the spiritual activity of the idea within nature as the living universal essence, and to understand the phenomena of the inorganic, organic and animated in the light of this all-embracing idea.

To Goethe, nature meant the artistic manifestation of the social organism of higher intelligences. And when looking at history, he was anxious to understand the general features and laws of the social organism of mankind as the result of individual activities, that is, of the will-impulses of the personality: "I have striven to understand the universal until I have learned to appreciate the particular attainments of distinguished men."

Information as to the results of Goethe's inquiries into natural phenomena can he found in various places. From the viewpoint that is suggested by a practicable sociology, one can consider here the answer to a particular question, which should be of interest to many: Can Goethe's method of research also give a new incentive to the social sciences after they have lost themselves in the darkness of mere outer observation, and the materialistic-statistical evaluations of social facts and activities?

The basic principles of Goethe's method must be found in his conviction that the scientific method that has proved successful for research in the realm of inorganic nature, cannot be applied to the domains of life existing beyond the lifeless. Goethe was aware that the human mind owes its clarity of consciousness, and ability to shape clear-cut thoughts, to the objective methods of physics and mathematics. And he knew also that these features have to be carried into a transformed exercise of knowledge. Only through such a metamorphosis can the successful basic method (of physical science) become fit for enquiring into the laws of higher realms of existence.

Goethe dared to apply the idea of metamorphosis to the development of scientific methods themselves. He transformed the method of *judging* the phenomena of the inorganic according to the law of outer cause and effect, into the method of *comparing* the incidental organic phenomena with the causative universal idea of organic life. Goethe proved that in organic nature the general *idea* is the supersensible cause of the particular and sensible effects. His method enabled him not only to conceive, but also even to perceive with his inner eye, this central idea as "entelechy," that is, as a creative entity.

Goethe himself did not succeed—and perhaps did not intend to—in grasping the central impulse of historic and social life in the same conceptual way he conceived and proved the reality of nature's ideas.[62] If one takes no account of Goethe's *Aphorisms*, one finds that in regard to human relationships he could have expressed his convictions only through his art, specifically through his *Faust* or in his fairy tale, *The Green Snake and the Beautiful Lily*, or in *Wilhelm Meister*. But in Goethe's method there lies also the potentiality of its further, higher development that permits, among other things, the scientifically conceived basic idea of social life.

Rudolf Steiner hinted at this fact with the words:

> ...I believe myself able to see that Goethe's ideas about the domains of nature, when experienced in their reality, must lead of necessity to the fruits of anthroposophical knowledge expounded by me. The ideas will lead there if one does what Goethe did not yet do: to carry the experiences made within the domain of nature towards those experiences to be made within the spiritual domain."[63]

It is in the spiritual domain that those ideas reside that manifest themselves within the human consciousness and become motives of action (ideals). They inspire the feeling and impart social aims to the will. In the form of moral ideas, the word of the spiritual world speaks directly to the

---

62   CHB: The same reservation belongs here as in footnote 61.

63   Rudolf Steiner, *Goethe's World View* (CW 6), *Mercury Press, Spring Valley, NY,* 1994.

human soul. Intuition is the inner faculty for the perception of moral ideas.

In the sense of Goethe's world conception and its development through anthroposophy it is not possible to establish a truly practical social science if the observing and reporting of outer facts, and the theoretical formulation of their laws, are not supplemented by methodical observation and cognition of spiritual life. Without consciously coming into contact with the spiritual domain it will not even be possible to form a true concept of "capital."[64] The essence of capital cannot be recognized by notions that merely refer to an amount of money, a collection of means of production, or to an interest-bearing investment.

But the true idea of capital can be formed through experiencing the organizing power of human intelligence and will as activating forces within the economic sphere, and the using of such outer means for the benefit of the social whole. How would it be possible to understand human actions, social intercourse, and cultural activities if, by the interplay of spiritual observation and the forming of suitable concepts, the mode of thinking, the forces of feeling, and the essence of will impulses inherent in the individuality were not fully understood in their social significance?

---

64 BB: This sentence would be entirely misunderstood if it were to lead a reader not acquainted either with true Goetheanism or with the fundamentals of anthroposophy to the far-fetched conclusion that only anthroposophists can form a true concept of "capital." The phenomenon of "capital" as the socially responsible spiritual activity of the individuality in the economic sphere—implemented through physical means—leads ordinary consciousness to the acceptance of *supersensible forces working in social life. Thus, the concept "capital," not polluted by subjective political emotions, can lead to contact with the spiritual domain in the Goetheanistic and anthroposophical sense, as does the experiencing of the life of any true idea.*

The "particular"—that is, the individual human being—can only be considered as a threefold entity composed of body, soul and spirit. As soon as man is recognized as such an entity, the general form of the social organism and its laws will also be recognized. The latter will appear as laws that man imposes upon himself first, and by means of which he determines the shape of the social organism by virtue of his self-controlled social activity. Thus does true freedom manifest itself. This spiritual freedom does not contradict our cherished ideal of liberty. On the contrary, the former, in its fundamental social meaning, fulfills the promise of the latter and protects it from being an empty phrase. Therefore, the social sciences such as history, ethnography, psychology, political science, sociology and economics are nothing but variations of the "science of freedom," as Rudolf Steiner called them when expounding the fundamentals of Goethe's world conception.

It is true that Goethe did not raise his method to a level that allowed him to express this truth scientifically. But his intuitive self-knowledge and world-observation prepared his mind in such a way that it could be and was touched and stirred by this idea. He experienced within his innermost being the organic interplay of thinking, feeling, and willing. These three soul forces were to him the individual representatives of exalted cosmic powers, and he depicted them in *The Green Snake and the Beautiful Lily*.

There they appear as the images of three kings: the golden king of wisdom, the silver king of beauty, the bronze king of goodness. They have taken up their abode in a subterranean treasure-cave, which suggests an image of the mysterious depths of the subconscious. But the call, "*The time is at hand*," sounds forth powerfully through the events narrated in the fairy tale. The hidden temple emerges from the darkness and rises to the surface of the earth. The three exalted cosmic forces have entered the conscious soul of man and manifest themselves in the daylight of social life as the true wellspring of spiritual rejuvenation.

At the same time, the stream of life is bridged over by the self-sacrifice of the Green Snake, an image by means of which Goethe wishes to convey the idea of human life-experience that has overcome egotism and dogmatism, and that has sacrificed itself in order to form this bridge between man and the world of the *Beautiful Lily*, representing the world of *ideas*. But in consequence of his own life-experience and his careful watching of events, Goethe is fully aware of social confusion in the world. He realized the existence of a fourth king, who is composed of a conglomerate of the above-mentioned three metals. This represents the general, fateful confusion arising out of a wrong relationship to one another of thinking, feeling and willing. It is the consequence of egotism mixed up with abstract and dogmatic generalizations, on the one hand, and struggle for power, on the other.

Goethe describes the total break-up of this king-of-confusion. This happens at the very moment when the exalted threefold kingdom of mankind becomes established. At this moment, when man has gained control of himself and of his three soul-forces, he starts to tackle the social problem. He is in conscious communication with the spirit. His work aims at the realization of the three ideals of modern mankind: freedom, equality, and brotherhood. This was the answer that Goethe gave to the central human question raised by the French Revolution: *How is it possible to make these three ideals work in a way that is practicable?*

The social impulse that was manifested through Goethe's magnificent imaginations was carried down into the conceptual sphere of natural science by Rudolf Steiner, who presented it as the idea of the threefold constitution of the human organism. He demonstrated how the threefold inner being of man is, during earthly life, supported by an organism that is likewise threefold. The supersensible inner being leans, to a certain extent, on the bodily sense-nerve system, with the consequence that objective ideas can become conscious in the subjective field.[65] Man's feeling is supported by the rhythmic, breathing system in connection with the circulation of blood, with the result that feelings can be experienced with the intensity of dream consciousness. The subconscious will is connected with the bodily functions of the third system, which works through metabolism in connection with the limbs. Man is the measure of all things. He is formed after the cosmic measures of nature, and he shapes the social organism through all that he makes his own, spiritually and in freedom, within the universal range of these measures.

The social organism therefore is a threefold one also, and lives through the right interplay of spiritual life, rights life and economic order. If, under the rule of the "conglomerate king," the interplay of the three domains of social life becomes inharmonious and the relative independence of each is disturbed, the social organism becomes sick. It is here that the true cause of the present disintegration of social life becomes evident. Only by promoting a healthy cooperation

---

65 How opposite this is to the social scientific convention that human beings are subjective creatures that need to be treated as "noise" excluded and demeaned as *homo economicus.* —ED.

among the three domains, through a full realization of their true nature, can the social life of mankind be rescued from the danger of complete annihilation.

The reassuring idea of the threefold social order must be recognized and realized; there is absolutely no other way. Through Goethe's supreme art, this idea has been heralded. Rudolf Steiner discovered it in the course of his methodical development of a true spiritual science. He embodied this idea in crystal-clear concepts, and verified them by clarifying and illuminating the deeper meaning of historical facts in the light of this idea. He discovered it in that Spirit of Truth Who has manifested Himself also through Goethe. To this Spirit, Goethe has paid homage with the words: "Wisdom is only in Truth."

As much as Goethe admired the technical discoveries that led to the Industrial Revolution, and have lately inspired United States' energy to accelerate the technicalization of social life, he was nevertheless fully aware of the dangers lurking in the future. In his *Wilhelm Meister,* we find the words:

> The rapid growth of machinery torments and frightens me; it is drawing near like a thunderstorm, slowly, slowly, but it has taken its direction; it will be here and it will strike.... People think and talk about it, but neither thinking nor talking will help. And who would like to imagine such terrors...?
>
> Only a twofold way is left, the one being as sad as the other; either we seize upon what is new, thus accelerating the disaster, or we start to seek a favorable destiny beyond the seas, and take along with us the best and the most worthy. Both ways are doubtful, but who may help us to weigh the reasons that should determine our actions?

Goethe's "beyond the seas" is the United States.[66] Times have changed. The United States can no longer offer refuge to all those "best and most worthy" who want to escape the consequences of the unsolved social question. The social problem has grown into a world problem, which now includes that of the United States' own salvation.[67] Goethe's struggle for true social values, and Rudolf Steiner's ideas about how to obtain them, should be recognized also in America as a most efficient spiritual help "to weigh the reasons that should determine our actions."

Auguste Comte (1798–1857), the father of sociology and positivism,[68] outlined a system of science and saw in its further development an exalted ideal of mankind. The base of his pyramid of sciences is formed by natural science, the apex is supposed to be sociology. Comte, who was influenced by the materialistic way of thinking, could only imagine that the well-tried method of physics could be extended into all other fields of inquiry, including social life. Sociology, therefore, was, to him, "social physics."

The system of sciences that Goethe started to build up and that Rudolf Steiner established, offers a social science based upon a metamorphosis of method that conforms with

---

66 This idea comes from Wolf Franck's paper, "Goethe for America." Op. cit. See footnote 12.

67 To what does "salvation" refer? —ED.

68 Positivism is a philosophical school that holds that all genuine knowledge is either true by definition or positive—meaning a posteriori fact derived by reason and logic from sensory experience. Other ways of knowing, such as intuition, introspection, or religious faith, are rejected or considered meaningless (*source*: Wikipedia). In other words, the idea that because something can be thought or done, it is validated by simply being thought or done. In the guise of economic positivism, especially regarding monetary behavior, this is precisely the battle that confronts anyone seeking to further Steiner's ideas in economics. —ED.

the nature of the particular subject in question. The system grows in an organic way from the metamorphosis of method. Therefore, it is crowned by a sociology that teaches the truth concerning man as a being endowed with the aptitude to be a free creator of the social organism. The base of this Goethean system is formed by a knowledge that makes intelligible the past evolution of man as a creature. In both cases, a knowledge of human nature is the starting point of science, and also the motive of action. In the archetype of man, these two [opposite] manifestations of human existence (thinking and willing) are united. The idea of man is the very heart of the social organism as the sun is the heart of our cosmic organism.

It was this idea that Goethe sought and that it was his desire to teach to mankind to the full capacity of his insight and abilities. A universal *Humanus* was Goethe's ideal. Thus, his work means: a social power that wishes to act only through the liberation of the human spirit and out of the fructification of the forces of the human individuality. *The peaceful, and peace promoting, power of spiritual initiative.*

7

Conditions Vital to the Social Organism

The so-called process of elimination, well-known to science, consists in gradually excluding all factors that, according to external observation and experiment, may modify the phenomenon in question but cannot be its decisive cause. What remains then reveals itself as the true cause, the primal phenomenon.

Today, we are experiencing in the destiny of mankind just such a process, applied by a Higher Intelligence on a gigantic scale. Through the configuration of historical facts, plan after plan for a new social order is tested for its truth and potentiality, carried *ad absurdum,* and rejected if not in conformity with the spirit of the time. There is but one idea compatible with this spirit; and social existence demands inexorably that this idea be received into our consciousness and our sense of responsibility as the primal phenomenon of our epoch.

The social catastrophes with their ever-growing destructive fury reveal themselves, in their sequence, as just such an agonizing process of elimination. Errors, half-truths, nebulous wishful thinking and abstract programs are discarded as clashing with reality. The more obstinately delusion clings to such distorted products of the human mind, and the more arrogant might be endeavors to enforce their realization, the more dearly mankind pays for the ultimate disillusionment. Only then, in the desert of annihilation, will the field be clear for the vision of the primal phenomenon.

Vast treasures of human and natural resources could be preserved from destruction and rendered fruitful for the rejuvenation of social life if the only idea capable of bringing salvation were mentally perceived and practically realized by a sufficient number of people. This central idea is that of the threefold ordering of the social organism, as conceived by Rudolf Steiner out of a profound spiritual knowledge of history-shaping impulses, and tirelessly promulgated during and after the First World War. As a social ideal, it shines like a sun in this midnight hour of mankind, a mankind that once before failed to accept it (writing close to the end of the Second World War). And today its light becomes brighter, more human—and more lonely— in proportion as the abyss of perdition yawns deeper and blacker.

The following sketch is a modest attempt to help men become aware of the idea of the threefold order as the true social impulse of our time, by considering the present situation of mankind from various points of view. If the reader can experience this impulse it will show us the way out of the abyss; and it will the more vividly awaken within us the will to cooperate in the shaping of the social life, the more we seek to re-discover it as the spiritual impulse in the scientific, artistic and religious lifework of Rudolf Steiner.

General[69]

The life and healthy development of an organism call for conditions of existence that accord with its nature. For natural organisms, such conditions are given. Where a plant germinates, grows, blossoms and bears fruit, where an animal is born, finds its nourishment and can propagate, the natural surroundings offer the conditions that enable such organic manifestations of life to come into being and to develop according to their own inner laws.

Man, as well, in so far as he is a natural organism, depends for his earthly life upon what nature offers; but he is not a nature-being only. He finds his proper conception of himself and his mission precisely in freely confronting nature, and in endeavoring to determine his relation to her out of his consciousness. In the course of his natural and historical development, he has more and more broken away from nature; and in so doing, he has risen to a plane on which, in accordance with the innate law of his being, he cooperates with her in creating conditions under which he can live.

This conscious cooperation in shaping the conditions of his earthly life has established such a relationship between man and fellow man that a new realm above nature has arisen: human society, or the social organism. In this organism the impulses of will, of emotional life and of thought tend to organize a social structure that, together with nature and as her essential complement, furnishes the conditions for the life of the individual. And the more clearly man divines the character of the substances and forces of nature, and learns to master their laws, the more conspicuously social coherence stands out as a new soil for human

---

69 Subheadings added to aid digestion of a long paper. —Ed.

existence in contrast to the old soil of nature. But since it is man himself who erects the social structure of his existence in association with his fellow men, he is confronted today by the most serious problem of this existence. The social organism has at present taken on a form that must convince even the most superficial observer that the forces now emanating from the human being are no longer those of conservation and construction, but of dissolution and destruction. One may ask: Has the social organism, as historically evolved, an innate law whose fulfillment depends upon man's awareness of it, and upon the degree of responsibility with which he faces his surroundings? Condensing this cardinal question of our time: What are the conditions vital to the social organism that the human being of today must consider in shaping his individual life in relation to his surroundings?

From Blood to Ego Family

The material preservation of an aggregation of human beings calls for sufficient food, clothing and shelter, and these are procured by working upon nature. Her products and raw materials are converted by labor into commodities suitable for human consumption. When such an aggregation organizes the work upon nature through the division of labor, an economic community comes into being. One essential condition of the life of the social organism is then, clearly, the necessity for satisfying the economic needs of the members of such a group by efficient division of labor and appropriate distribution.

A glance at history, particularly at the more recent presentations of prehistoric cultures and scientific researches into the mode of life of the so-called "primitives," reveals the fact that the formation of groups solely for the purpose of better satisfying economic needs is not to be found. Neither the history of the past nor an examination of the present discloses anywhere or at any time a purely economic community as a social organism. Only such social forms can be discovered whose coming into existence implies, in addition to their economic activity, the presence of quite different forces—community-building forces. Indeed, in mankind's past it was just these other, non-economic, connections that made a common economic life possible.

Quite aside from the fact that the present scientific concepts concerning aboriginal mankind are in need of revision, the primeval family cannot be explained by the animal instinct of mating and the urge of reproduction alone; nor is it imaginable as a mere economic community in which father and sons hunted while mother and daughters managed the household. It was first of all a community held together by soul and spirit. From the basis of common blood grew the feeling of belonging together, while identical experiences of nature yielded a common knowledge of participation in a spirit-pervaded cosmos. Upon this community feeling and these experiences rested also the possibility of a common economic activity; and what is true in a narrow sense of the family applies equally to the tribe in a wider sense. It is quite obvious that owing to the same descent, members of a tribe considered themselves a soul-spiritual community through which the same blood flowed and common ancestors spoke. The religious attitude of man toward his ancestors and toward the spiritually experienced being of nature was at the same time the source of law; and religion and law together furnished the foundation by which the economic life was regulated.

Wherever our retrospective glance encounters peoples entering the stream of history in larger social units, we find a diminution in the awareness of a common blood and of the ancestor and nature-consciousness bound up with it. More and more, it is superseded by the consciousness of a cultural tradition, of a common language, of a folk-individuality with a mission for the future—in short, of a higher spiritual life; and this in turn gives meaning and form to the rights life as well as to the economic order. In the remote past, the social organism with its three basic functions was identical with the family-community—or with the community united as a tribe of blood-related families; but in the course of evolution it transformed itself into the people, whose members felt their folk-unity enclosed within fixed geographical boundaries much more strongly than did the old family and tribal communities.

Evolution did not stop with this: peoples transformed themselves into nations. The social organism in the form of a nation draws its life-forces far more from the individual consciousness than is the case with a people, for the latter is still close to the old collective consciousness. As a nation, it develops a national consciousness, in the sense that the individual strives to take into his personal consciousness the spiritual essence of the people, and to realize this through his will in an individual way. Upon this basis of consciousness, the spiritual life of the nation develops. Individual identification with the national Spirit becomes the prime criterion of membership. Not the identity of blood is the determining factor, but rather the identity of mentality evolved independently of physical heredity, and the will to fulfill certain conditions laid down by law. The fact that a person is born within the frontiers of a nation—that is, the place where he was born—is usually decisive in recognizing his citizenship. Whenever the law stipulates for such recognition that he be born of citizens of the nation in question, this is only a faint echo of the sense of blood-related communities; for it is not the purity of the parents' blood that counts, but only the external consideration of their inherited or acquired citizenship.

Individual perception of the duty to cooperate with all others in the development of the nation's rights life, coupled with the need to harmonize it with individual demands, is the source of the democratic impulse. This becomes the decisive factor in forming the state, in the modern sense of the word. On the other hand, the individual choice of profession and the consequent need of specialized training become characteristic of an economic life that unfolds within the boundaries of a nation and rests upon a division of labor carried out ever more consciously.

The social forms we have described shape the existence of many parallel social organisms. Each derives its life-force from a historically developed spiritual, rights and economic life, and it unfolds within a definite geographic region. The social organism in its historically evolved form has, as it were, its own external domain, its *Lebensraum.*

Present-day man is obsessed by the idea that a nation, bounded by political frontiers, represents the highest development possible for the social organism. He believes that only by perfecting the social life within the nation, and by improving the relations of nations among each other, can future development be served. Few people notice that the being of the social organism is a living entity striving for a higher form of development that must inevitably blast the cultural, political and economic boundaries of the nation, endowing this nation with a mission within the framework of a greater unit—a mission it could never find within its own limited sphere. Whoever obstructs this trend of the social organism toward a new and up-to-date form contributes to the destruction of its vital conditions.

Economic Aspects

Since the end of the 19th century, man's economic activity has far outgrown national frontiers. The process of production has become international. The web of interrelated operations, leading finally to the finished product, extends over the globe. The preliminary stages of procuring raw materials and of producing one-quarter, one-half and three-quarters finished articles in the realm of modern industrialism show that in reality no single operation is determined by the character of a circumscribed economic field, but rather that only its technical connection with innumerable other operations makes it possible at all. These in their entirety bear an international character, and every influence brought to bear upon any single operation by the national organization—that is, by the national spiritual life or law—must necessarily influence the total international process of production as well. The same is true of the distribution and exchange of goods: they depend on world-traffic. In like manner, consumption no longer draws upon national economy, but upon the mass of social products offered by world-economy. This world economy, called into being since the end of the 19th century along with technical development, proves by the irrefutable logic of facts that the living evolutionary force in the social organism has expanded beyond national frontiers. This force has done away with these frontiers without thus far having found an arrangement in accord with its inherent impulse, yet an arrangement of that kind is a vital condition of the social organism in the present and the future.

Economic life tends toward worldwide expansion; any attempt to confine it within national boundaries by means of uncongenial legislation and a spiritual life misinterprets its essence and undermines its vital conditions. This makes the economic body into a disturbing element in the present and future development of mankind, thus forcing it into conflict with other economic bodies. If such conflicts, which must eventually lead to war, are to be prevented in the future, economic bodies that loom out of the past and that have grown on national soil must be transformed. They must be given a form that does not conflict with the international character of the modern interplay of production, distribution and consumption. Economic bodies must adopt a form tending to stimulate the development of a global economic order. Looked at from the viewpoint of world economy, mankind no longer manifests itself as an integrated number of peoples and nations, living side by side in geographically bounded regions and in more or less harmonious relations, but as a single social organism whose functions encompass the globe. If an organic economic order with fair distribution of community-produced social commodities is a vital condition of every circumscribed community, this is even more the case when a community life not bounded by nationality has emerged through the inexorable action of unleashed economic forces. Here we are confronted with an historical fact demanding recognition, true appraisal and full consideration in all future economic activity.

This leads to the question: What principle must be decisive in organizing future economic bodies and in the timely transformation of present ones? It can only be the principle of *association*. The economic association is demanded by modern division of labor itself as a counterpart and organic complement. Only through the principle of association can the impulses, active in the division of labor as determined by capital for the last three centuries, arrive at a final organic settlement compatible with their nature and socially justified. Heretofore this associative principle has not been given a chance to operate in the purely economic sense: it has been adulterated and diluted. Adulterated in that nationalistic impulses have given economic life its direction and that economic association has been sought for the purpose of increasing national power; and diluted through the materialistic conception of the nature of mankind, which concedes only community-economy as the single vital condition.

It is an historical fact that each single function of economic work is indissolubly connected with all the others; and when this is grasped the associative principle in its purity becomes clear. Then one will also understand the economic law affirming that a contribution can only be made to the social totality, and that therefore adequate sharing in the social product must be granted (reciprocated?) by the social totality as an equivalent.[70] A fundamental social law of that sort, however, does not operate like a law of nature without human agency: it grows out of historical evolution, and it can only be fulfilled through a full knowledge of its manner

---

70 Referring, presumably, to the fundamental social law and the social ethic. —ED.

of operation and through the fully conscious attitude of each single individual.

The branching out of the production process into ever more detailed and segregated part-functions, taken in conjunction with the ever-increasing demands of the machine age, calls for intelligent union of these part-functions. Just as no comprehensive science can result from analytical thinking without its synthetic counterpart, so no mere division of labor—or the combination of labor under uneconomic conditions—can ever yield an economic system equal to its tasks. Part-work is associated with part-work in order to achieve the greatest economic results with the least means; but let it be understood that by "the greatest results" is meant the best supply in quantity and quality—not the highest rate of interest on the capital invested.

As long as this associative principle is thought of as functioning only within isolated production activities, its essential nature is not understood. Its urge is rather to express itself in the entire economic system, reaching beyond the frame of the individual enterprise. Industries feel the need of association with each other because even these represent only a part-function of the total economic system. Whenever a finished product is turned out, concomitant economic facts call for an association with the manufacturers of similar products, with the suppliers of raw materials and of half-finished articles and accessories, as well as with the producers of the requisite machinery, and so forth. The same exigency demands an expertly controlled organic connection with trade, transport, communication, and especially with the banking business and the money system. Finally, through the associative principle in its universal application, an intelligent contact with the consumer becomes a necessity, keeping in view the best possible methods of supply and of price-determination.

Here a few further words are in order concerning the misapplication of the associative principle. One such, for example, can be seen in the usual methods of syndicates, rings and trusts. These as a rule seek amalgamation with, and centralized control of, similar or complementary industries for a purpose incompatible with a true associative total economy. Their aim is a monopolistic control of the market and of the price of a certain product or group of products. The forming of such pseudo-associations (better put, cartels?) purposes not the best possible means of supplying indispensable goods, but rather the highest rate of interest on the capital invested. The social damages to which this ambition has led have at the same time aggravated another equally baneful tendency; and incidentally, that same ambition, in the shape of egotistical, international power derived from capital, has always reached out across national frontiers and contributed in large measure to the creation of world-economic entanglements. The tendency referred to is government attempts first to supervise, then to direct, and finally to organize economic life.

Rights Life

The economic activity of man, even when worldwide, represents only one of his essential relations to his surroundings, hence an associative economic organization can fulfill only one vital condition of the social organism. Another expression of social intercourse takes the form of rights life. A well-developed stage of such a rights life comes to outer expression in the organization of the state, which logically cannot be derived from purely economic exigencies. Rights belong to another sphere of social life. Just as one cannot comprehend the human organism by trying to explain the breathing system by means of the nervous system, and vice versa,[71] but can arrive at a better understanding by examining the character of each and their cooperation, so the economic and the rights life cannot be derived one from the other, or the one built up out of the other. Both must be shaped out of a conscious perception of their peculiar characters and brought into realistic harmony. "Shaping" is here intended to signify the transformation of an historically given entity whose form no longer tallies with the spirit of the present; and this is true not only of the economic life but of the rights life as well.

The rights life has grown out of historical soil, and its germ is to be found in the kinship men felt in the remote past as a result of a common descent. Common blood was the source of this feeling, and social relations were regulated under the inspiration of the same Spirit who was experienced as active in the blood. One such regulation represents the law. The legislator was the one who could give to the blood-related community a system that was not only an organized entity but also the best timely expression of the common Spirit active through the generations. This principle in its most highly developed form achieved its purest expression in the Law of the Old Testament Hebrews.

In the course of historical evolution, the sense of kinship diminished in proportion as the mixing of blood superseded the preservation of pure blood, as had been demanded by the Law. The common experiencing of the Group-Spirit

---

71 A reference to the threefold nature of the human being discussed earlier. —ED.

dwindled, and in its place grew a more and more conscious experiencing of one's own individual being. The old blood-relationship was a given fact, not open to discussion. The new ego-consciousness furnished the soil upon which men could discuss the subject of right and wrong. The fading impulse of the blood-community was superseded by the new-born democratic impulse: in the train of the general metamorphosis of consciousness a change came over man's attitude toward the law and his awareness of it.

Upon this foundation of a new consciousness has grown the modern state with its parliamentary system. Its principle is that every adult is credited with the ability to distinguish between general and individual interests, as well as with the capacity to cooperate in developing legislation in the general interest, even if only by the election of suitable parliamentary representatives. Such a new rights life could at first develop only within the external framework of peoples and nations grown out of communities of blood-relationship and traditions; but this fact should not blind us to the true inner nature of the democratic impulse alive within it—or better, the *anthropocratic* impulse.[72]

The democratic impulse is a universal human impulse in national garb; and this garb has become too tight. One need only follow with an open mind the historical development and spread of democracy, from antiquity through the medieval state-forms up to the structure and constitutions of the European nations, in order to perceive that this impulse, in its form-giving force, cannot stop at the geographical and spiritual frontiers of a nation. Its sphere of action is mankind, a body in which nations and peoples

---

72 If this term is not to be an awkward one, it presumably means human beings recognizing (and respecting) one another as such. —ED.

are the organs through whose activity the individual human being is prepared for life within the social order in its highest sense. The separate organs of the human body remain incomprehensible as regards their special functions and structure, if the total function and form of the human organism is not taken into account. In like manner, the mission and the social form of a nation are revealed only through a grasp of the essence of mankind as a whole, which manifests itself spiritually in the individual man and has a socially constructive effect in the erection of a democratic rights life. Parliament was originally planned as a public assembly where the general feeling for right should be crystallized into a well-defined content of rights-consciousness—not, however, by the representation of selfish interests, but by the free discussion of individual minds. Who would seriously maintain today that the universal feeling for right, which is the source of justice emanating from the soul, should halt at national frontiers?[73]

All that was said concerning the course of development taken by the economic life—from the time when it was limited to groups and nations until it became a general world-economy—is equally applicable to the impulse of democratic rights tending in the same direction. Along a trail of catastrophes, democracy is on its way from a nationally bounded to a universal system of human rights: to an anthropocracy. One outstanding cause of such catastrophes is the fact that, owing to the tenacity of all nationally bounded feeling and thinking, the pace of democratic development is slower than the precipitate growth of economic life. Ever since the 17th century, when Grotius

---

73 CHB: The feeling, yes, but not its institutional embodiment.

proclaimed the freedom of the seas as a universal principle of law, thereby inaugurating the idea of an international legal system, a universal impulse toward justice has sought a form capable of organization. But time and again its development was stopped. The democratic sense of rights, which is independent of blood-ties, was adulterated by being side-tracked in the direction of obsolete, nationally selfish world-conceptions and interests.

To conclude from what has been set forth here, that the intellectualistic-programmatic construction of an abstract, general super-state is advocated vaguely to parallel the actuality of world-economy, would be to misunderstand it completely. There is no question here of doing away with the historically grown political structures of peoples, but of guiding history into a course in conformity with reality: by the perception and individual realization of the social motives that shape history. The question concerns the timely conditions under which these political structures can survive and peacefully carry their development into the future. Only under such practical, worldwide conditions as set forth [here] can peoples fulfill their specific economic and spiritual missions as organs of the organism of mankind without having to resort to arms in defense of the expansion of their place in the sun. All that is meant is that every legal code of every people, whose members are linked with all other peoples through world-economic as well as spiritual relations (more of this later), must be so fashioned as to express true democracy. Only thus can the latter become a unifying element, not only among members of the same nation, but most particularly an element uniting man with man, and thereby peoples with peoples as well. The creation of international institutions of law—courts of arbitration and the like—will then become a practicable matter relatively easy to put into effect.[74]

A code thus democratically shaped and conforming with the individual economic and cultural customs of the various peoples, but also with the demands of an associative world-economy, would yield practical results. No code would conflict with certain rights that everyone must demand under the present conditions of human existence, to whatever race or people he may belong.

The general acknowledgment of such rights and the specific incorporation of them in every political system would constitute the basis for fulfilling the second vital condition of the total social organism. Among such rights may be mentioned, for example:

a) In return for each individual piece of work done for the social totality, the right to participate in the general social product to an extent securing subsistence for the length of time required to produce the same article again. This is a question of rights and therefore law, not of economy.[75]

---

74 CHB: Again, one wonders. At the time of Behrens writing, in 1948 the General Agreement in Tariffs and Trade (GATT) was established to ease multilateral trade accords among the countries of the world—a global, yet articulated and not centralized arrangement. The United States and France averred otherwise, and in 1995 the World Trade Organization replaced the GATT with a uni-global institution with globally binding laws and its own court.

75 CHB: Without crediting it or saying so, this is again clearly a direct allusion to "the fundamental social law." But it is also reminiscent of Steiner's true price formula: "a 'true price' is forthcoming when a person receives, as counter-value for the product he has made, sufficient to enable him to satisfy the whole of his needs, including of course the needs of his dependants, until he will again have completed a like product." (*Economics*, lecture 6.) It is debatable, however, whether true prices are best arrived at from external or

The latter has here the obligation to fulfill the
conditions imposed upon it by law, which was
developed independently of it. It can accomplish
this only if its corporations enjoy a genuine
associative relation to each other.

b) The right to education, in the sense of free
development of individual abilities, together with
the right of free access to all cultural institutions.[76]

c) The right to combine with others for the
cultivation of common interests.[77]

Just as the economic order of a people must not conflict
with the associative principle of world-economy, so its legal
code must not oppose the international democratic impulse.
The desire to avoid such conflicts points at the same time
to the practical limits within which rights and economic
life can develop in harmony with the individual peculiar-
ity of a group of men—peoples, for example, or a group
of peoples. Such individual development of separate social
organisms would in addition represent an essential contribution toward the creation of the conditions vital to the
social organism as a whole.

---

inherent regulation, from external laws or the logic of associative
economic conduct. The impositions of basic incomes or minimum
wages provide a case in point.

76 SV: Note that right of access is not the same as a right to determine
the form and the content of education.

77 SV: The First Amendment to the United States Constitution, for
example, states: "Congress shall make no law...abridging the
freedom of speech, or of the press; or the right of the people
peaceably to assemble..."

A Free Spiritual Life

Man shall not live by bread alone, nor is his conception of his own possibilities exhausted by his consciousness of belonging to a people. To his economic and his rights relations with his fellowmen must be added a third: the spiritual. This is intrinsically a spiritual relation. Out of man's spiritual relation to his surroundings—and to himself—grows a knowledge of the world and of man in the form of science, art and religion. Art endeavors to impart an individual expression of truth, and through religion man can experience the spiritual unity of human and cosmic being. As the expressions of the true, the beautiful and the good respectively, science, art and religion constitute in their interrelation the foundation upon which man erects the temple of true culture. In its halls, he can live as a free spirit and meet with other free spirits. Here is the true wellspring for the education of the younger generation; and here, too, man works at his own individual development through self-knowledge, self-control and self-transformation. It is the holy place from which he looks back upon nature and, by contemplating her kingdoms and forms, divines the first steps in the evolution of mankind. Here he seeks to comprehend the course of history as the path trodden by man as he rose out of nature to ever-higher planes of consciousness, and to recognize the field of history as the sphere of increasingly conscious motives of action. Here he sees the kingdom of man being added to the kingdoms of nature as a social realm, and as the result of his own purposeful activity. This temple of true culture is at the same time a high watchtower, enabling man not only to view the past and fathom its meaning, but to divine his future mission in the form of moral motives. Their realization spells the history to come, as well as the transformation of the social organism into a higher form.

The right fostering of cultural life is not only the third external vital condition of the social organism, but also the highest and purest inner source of social life itself. The force permeating it out of the spiritual realm is to the social organism what nourishment is to the natural organism. During the time of their rise and flowering, the old folk cultures were permeated by just such spiritual forces. Under their influence, members of the same people experienced themselves as children of the same Folk-Spirit. Those folk-cultures were the preliminary steps by which man in his historical evolution rose to the consciousness of his own individuality.

In the shaping of a national spiritual life within the frame of the state, developing after the close of the Middle Ages upon a democratic foundation and through the industrializing of economic life, a struggle between two forces is clearly in evidence. One of these is the personality, conscious of independence and of self, which employs its acquired political liberty, takes advantage of the disappearance of outmoded economic forms, and discards untenable creeds for the purpose of shaping economic life, government and education in accord with the newly found world-feeling. In the course of this process, it becomes ever clearer that these three activities are governed by forces transcending national considerations. We have already pointed to this in connection with the associative impulse of economy and the democratic impulse of legislation. Natural science—which is the foundation in the educational field—also refuses to be confined within national boundaries. It has long since blasted these; for through the spatial extent of its field of interest, as well as through the method and form of presenting its results, it has become an international power.

The other conflicting force strives to obstruct the international, universal unfolding of these three activities, to limit their sphere of influence to the area of the nation. The spiritual past of a people has become mere tradition, yet it is substituted by force, as it were, and by the power of suggestion for the immediate experiencing of the fateful situation in which mankind now finds itself. To a spiritual life that in its materialistic structure has become dependent upon external sense-perceptions, this situation must remain obscure. The state—which during the time of its birth and adolescence received its formative forces from a vivid spiritual life but that, in consequence of the social sterility of materialistic mental life, now finds only dead tradition to work with— revives this in an unwholesome manner. It incorporates the institutions of the spiritual life in its administration, and imparts to them an anachronistic line of development unrelated to actuality.

Spiritual life loses its freedom at the moment when standing in greatest need of it as a new foundation—that is, at the moment when man awakens to the consciousness and mental grasp of his individuality. The scientist, the artist, the priest become servants of the state. They become officials. Within the framework of a spiritual life administered or decisively influenced by government, the citizens' soul and spirit are molded along the lines of the political party in power at the moment. The democratic right of the individual to education, meaning the development of his special aptitudes in the universal human sense, is canceled by the presumption of government in determining this education in terms of narrow political ideas. Added to this, either directly or indirectly through government, the economic life assigns tasks to the spiritual life that exhaust its strength in research and invention of a technical and economic nature—harnessing them only for the purpose of raising the purely external standard of living. In many countries, even religion is more and more supervised by a bureaucratic government. All this must be viewed in the light of the fact that since the decline of medieval culture, which had grown out of a purely spiritual soil, the social organism has produced no *new* culture. It has merely developed an admirable technical science. But the results of natural science cannot satisfy the longing for a solution of the deeper problems of human existence: that the methods of this natural science have led the human spirit to the very threshold of an inner freedom, at which lies the starting-point of the metamorphosis of natural science into a genuine {because} spiritual science—something that has been noticed only by Rudolf Steiner.

Right up to the immediate present man has nourished soul and spirit with the remains of past spirit-imbued cultures, and now he is anxious: everything is consumed; the cupboard is empty; the *horror vacui* grips him. Out of the great void sounds forth the question: How shall I once more find the source from which flow those spiritual impulses indispensable to the life of the social organism? To experience this question with the full power of the soul is the prerequisite of finding the answer. Just as every individual must purge his own inner being of selfish interests and dogmatic concepts if the spirit is to reveal itself to him in the form of imagination, inspiration and intuition, so, too, must science, art and religion be purged of the litter of economic and political interests, government interference and dogmatism. The well-spring of spiritual life will then flow forth again, and its waters will no longer be polluted by civilization's refuse that must be eliminated from the social organism as something indigestible.

The call is for a truly free spiritual life, and its administration, independent of government and the economy, must be erected upon its own soil in conformity with its own being. In the human organism, the metabolic system is functionally marked off quite clearly from the rhythmic system on the one hand and from the nervous-sensory system on the other, only thereby being enabled to serve as the vehicle for nourishing the organism as a whole. In like manner, the social organism can obtain pure spiritual nourishment only from a spiritual life untouched by extraneous interests.

Social Existence as a Task

The three conditions vital to the social organism as referred to here can be understood in their deeper significance only by those who can hear the demand for their realization being fairly shouted from the tumultuous chaos of the present. One such demand is the assurance of a standard of living in keeping with human dignity. What can this mean other than the longing for an associatively shaped economic life, without which this age of industrialism is bound to bring over- or under-production with its consequent uneconomic, vacillating prices and social pauperization?

Another demand to be heard on all sides is for removing the possibility now enjoyed by economic and political power-groups (lobbies) to influence the form of government and the judicial realm in the pursuit of their selfish interests. What can this mean but a demand for the unobstructed development of the democratic impulse through an independent rights life?

The third and loudest cry is for a creative idea of culture that can be incorporated in the will of all through education, the arts and the impetus of true religion by way of every individual consciousness. Only through a free spiritual life can this demand be satisfied.

A practical threefold ordering of the social organism satisfies the three fundamental demands of our time, and its execution fulfills the conditions under which mankind can survive and develop as a social organism. Man receives his own natural organism through birth: it is given him as the result of past evolution. But the social organism is given him not as a fruit, but as a task. He can no longer entrust the control of his very own realm to unreliable instincts or to a nebulous notion of so-called progress. He himself must beget a social organism in the womb of the present antisocial chaos; but the procreative force lies in the true idea of the social organism that is kindled in the individual consciousness and raised through free will to an ideal—that is, to the motive of action in the three separate realms of social existence.

The United States' Special Circumstances

The War-catastrophe engulfing us writes its *Memé-Tékêl*[78] with flaming letters on the dark background of the world-tempest; and though it appears to be a warning only for whole peoples, it is in reality directed toward every single human being. Peoples cannot be called to account:

---

78   Daniel's "writing on the wall." —Ed.

responsibility is placed by the destiny of the time upon each human being. The weight of this burden will depend upon one's judgment; and by this scale will one be judged by a higher court.

It should be easy for a United States citizen to grasp the deeper meaning of the threefold ordering of social life from what has here been sketchily suggested. Of all the peoples of the earth, the people of the United States has the briefest tradition, hence it should be least embarrassed by it or by deep rooted customs. Its short history, which is the history of modern technical development, proves that the people of the United States are *par excellence* the people of rapidly changing habits. Slowness within the material life is an unknown concept in the United States. Such states of inertia as, for instance, the sense of affinity created by common blood, have played a secondary role or none at all in the development of a people and a nation out of a community of colonists.[79]

Probably every people on earth has contributed through immigration to the folk-substance of the United States and the building up of the nation. In view of the peculiar process of its birth and the development of its civilization, constitution and economy, the people of the United States might paradoxically be called a universal nation. It owes its coming into being and its development to a world-constellation that, since the end of the Middle Ages that came to a close with the discovery of the Americas, not only transformed Europe, but really created the United States in the field of modern history. It could only have been this predestined internationalism (meaning an historical reality, not an abstract program) that offered the healthy, fresh soil for the reception

---

79 CHB: Meaning "white" settlers, for the people of other ethnicities do not typically rush or exhibit individualism.

and further development of the democratic ideal born in the Old World. It is precisely through a fully conscious grasp of the idealistic human forces in the United States, reaching out beyond the national frontiers, that the democratic ideal can be carried toward its ever-purer realization. Selfish, nationalistic forces are opposed to the nature of the people of the United States; hence such forces must inevitably obstruct the further development of the true democratic impulse.

All this goes to show that the (true) war aim of the people of the United States can only be a peace that will bring democracy to everybody, giving everyone the right to participate in determining the form of government under which he intends to live.

Economic life in the form of modern industrialism has reached its climax in the United States. Within an amazingly short time (part of) a gigantic continent has been transformed into the foundation of a unified economic body. Nowhere else could the individual power of labor and organization have developed so freely as on this (middle area of this northern part of this) continent between the Atlantic and the Pacific.[80] For 450 years, there was unlimited room to live and act for anyone willing to work (provided they acquired the land of those there before them). The founding and developing of a democratic federal system was relatively easy in a community extending over many thousand square miles as long as the economy, through its far-reaching development and expansion to the West, remained on the upward curve. But around the turn of the century the westward drive came to an end. The boundary-line was reached. The economic life of

---

80 CHB: It may feel like a point is being labored, but supra-assertion of the United States is simply something that has to be remedied, and by the people of the United States themselves.

the United States could no longer expand spatially. Its forces now streamed back into the interior, compelling intensification through economic organization. Industrialism became ever more potent, producing new and unforeseen problems for democracy; and these become more pressing in proportion as the importance of exports exceeds that of imports. In the matter of exports, industrial products take their place beside farm products in importance, implying a tightening of economic interrelations, particularly since capital has become an export article.

The axis of world-trade has now shifted, owing to the increased speed of vessels and the use of airborne transportation of merchandise. The route from Europe to Asia runs increasingly via the United States, which will soon no longer be "the West," but in the language of traffic and economy will have to be called the *central continent* between Asia and Europe. Asia's millions await full economic development; the European millions, economic reconstruction. Geographical position and a highly developed economy will of necessity determine the United States' own tasks within the future world-economy. These it will not be able to fulfill out of a self-sufficient isolationism, but only through the practical association of the United States economy with other economic bodies.

But the prerequisite of such a worldwide economic association is that the United States' economic life be enabled to make its own contribution to the solution of its own (domestic) social problems. Within its own sphere, it must carry out the associative principle, independent of government interference and political interests, and unmolested by narrow ideological tendencies, if it is to achieve adequate supply and appropriate price-levels. Precisely because the United States has always been the "Promised Land" of economic initiative, the spirit of enterprise can here best be given the direction toward an associative organization of economy. It was only the economic crisis after 1929 and the exigencies of war that forced the government to take a hand in guiding the economy, in the absence of any economic order adequately meeting industrial demands. In the time granted it between Versailles and the outbreak of the current war, ravaged Europe failed to solve the social problem in the only way worthy of human intelligence. It needs an example of how a democratic rights life comprising 48 federated states[81] can cooperate with an associatively organized continental economy. Without such an exemplary solution of the home social problems the most beautiful program for the re-organization of Europe will necessarily remain ineffectual. Only such an example can stimulate the individual forces of goodwill to find in Europe a social form compatible with its own economic, political and cultural conditions. That is the second war-aim that can offer a permanent basis for peace.[82]

The United States has always accorded freedom to spiritual life. The early immigrants sought more than the opportunities offered for free economic and political activities: persecuted on religious grounds, they came over primarily in search of spiritual liberty.[83] On the one hand, the spiritual

---

81 In 1959, Alaska and Hawaii were added. —ED.

82 CHB: It has to be asked, however, where in this concept of Europe does the UK stand, for this was rarely a reference for the English? What, in other words, does Behrens make of the "special relationship"?

83 CHB: This is surely not the case. The "discovery" of North America was about relaxing the prevention of European humanity going there prematurely. Religious liberty is but an aspect of this and in no wise its equal.

life of the United States rises from the springs of numerous religious faiths and philosophies of countless shades: a motley spiritual life lacking all unity. On the other hand, a uniform but colorless natural-scientific activity has developed. Between these two facets of our spiritual life an external relationship appears to exist, in that parishes, religious sects and the like endeavor to clothe their religious life in a sort of scientific garment; while in science, especially psychology, certain tendencies to incorporate the religious factor become increasingly manifest, though also more futile. Something that is conspicuous at a glance, however, as an influence in education and teaching, doctrine and research, is the economic aim of it all. In general, most research is for purely utilitarian purposes, and nearly all education is for merely personal ends, with knowledge sought only for its economic value, education for raising economic efficiency. The spiritual life, though free to a high degree in its form, is so obscured in its true being by a conceptual life developed under the spell of economy that its essential content is rendered impotent.

When the proper cultural tasks of the spiritual life are thus obscured, the latter can unfold no really constructive activity within its own field. Its life-forces are absorbed by the economic body. Hypertrophy of economic life confronts atrophy of the spiritual life.

Here we encounter the problem of a newly born United States' culture, which alone can endow the United States' form of civilization with a true spiritual content. By this is meant a culture not sustained by European traditions brought over, or by imported Asiatic ones, but rather the carrying on and cultivation of European culture-impulses by spiritually free personalities upon virgin soil,[84] under perfected democratic and more favorable economic conditions. Were Asia to perceive the timely unfolding of a genuine culture of personality within a free spiritual life radiating towards it across the Pacific, this would not appear particularly strange to an Asian person. He would divine in such a culture transcending nationalism the social resurrection of the ancient Asiatic spiritual impulses that helped shape Europe after their metamorphosis through Antiquity and the Middle Ages. To open the way for the spirit in its manifestation through free individuality should be the third aim of a struggle intended to lead to true peace.

The struggle in which destiny inevitably involves the United States has thrown old forms of human organization into chaos. Only if a sufficient number of people raise the true idea of mankind in its threefold activity to an ideal can the seed of a healthy social organism be planted in the chaos of the present.

---

84   CHB: How so, "virgin soil"?

8

Death and Life of Democracy

Until the end of the 19th century, democracy was an expanding principle. After being foreshadowed in antiquity, it began to unfold in England in the 17th century and came to full expression in the French Revolution and in the constitution of the United States. The 19th century was a triumphal march for it.

This triumphant expansion came to a sudden end in the first half of the 20th century. The democratic states were reduced to a minority position and forced to fight for their existence. The majority of men lost their faith in the democratic impulse and in its significance for the future. They sought to replace democratic government by other principles of group-life. This change was accomplished not by physical force alone, but also by the weight of the arguments put forward by the enemies of democracy. The prevailing consciousness was unable to see the fallacies in these arguments.

It is the condition of their consciousness that determines how the members of a group create a legal form or correspond to the forcible imposition of such a form. Our actions, our relations to our fellow-men, are governed by the way in which we experience ourselves and by our attitude toward our physical environment, our group, and the domain of the spiritual. Our awareness of human rights is an important factor in our consciousness. In the course of time it has changed, causing alterations in political forms. Parallel changes in other aspects of our consciousness have caused alterations in spiritual life and economic activity.

Have our consciousness and our relation to the world changed so profoundly in this century that the democratic idea is no longer valid? Must we regard democracy as the dying creation of an antiquated consciousness? If this is correct, what are the traits of the new consciousness, and what legal form(s) will correspond to it?

The Origins of and Challenges to Democracy

Democracy originated among men whose consciousness was similar to ours,[85] but not identical. In ancient Athens, "government by the people" did not mean what it means to us. For us, a "people" means the totality of the persons in a group who are united by their mutual, unique, historically evolved ties in the field of culture, rights and economy. In ancient Athens, however, only the "free" men were full citizens. This meant primarily those who owned property. Serfs and slaves were not included.

The slave was the *object* of legal rights. As subject, he had no part in legislation, administration or elections. He was a part of the people in the broad sense, but was excluded from the people in a particular sense, i.e., from the political life. How closely this is connected with consciousness can be seen from Aristotle's attitude toward slavery. Aristotle regarded the existence of a slave-caste as a necessity of nature. For him, the distinction between master and slave proceeded not

---

85 Presumably, referring to citizens of the United States. —Ed.

so much from external power as from their different attitudes toward the *spirit*:

> Where then there is such a difference as that between soul and body, or between man and animals (as in the case of those whose business is to use their body, and who can do nothing better), the lower sort are by nature slaves, and it is better for them as for all inferiors that they should be under the rule of a master. For he who can be, and therefore is, of another's, and he who participates in rational principle enough to apprehend, but not to have, such a principle, is a slave by nature. Whereas the lower animals cannot even apprehend a principle; they obey their instincts. It is clear, then, that some men are by nature free, and others slaves and that, for these latter, slavery is both expedient and right. (*Politics,* book I, chapter 5)

Here the unequal legal relation is traced back to an unequal relation to the spirit. Only the free men because of their equality before the spirit can live within the sphere of political equality, i.e., democracy. Political equality comes from spiritual freedom. In an external sense, freedom was possible at that time only through the existence of the slaves. As Hegel pointed out in his *Philosophy of History*:

> In Athens, Sparta, etc., the various trades and businesses were given over to the slaves. Thus, the free men were not cumbered with differences in occupation and education and could maintain themselves in fuller equality. Slavery was necessary for such a beautiful democracy, where every citizen had the right and duty of delivering and hearing lectures on government in the public square, exercising in the gymnasiums, participating in the festivals.... The equality of the citizens entailed the exclusion of the slaves.

Thus, in pre-Christian times freedom was not for mankind in general, but was confined to the elect. The Logos sojourned in spiritual heights, having not yet descended to the depths of earthly existence. Since the earth had not yet been made the body of the Logos, there was no meaning in the saying: "He who eats my bread treads upon Me with his feet." As long as bread was baked by slaves, the mystery of a fraternal economy lay far in the future. Hence, in his *Republic* Plato looks to the oriental caste-system as the ideal political arrangement.

In antiquity, philosophical thinking, reaching toward the Logos, who dwelt still in spiritual heights, was advancing toward individual freedom, but was unable to grasp this concept in its entirety. Philosophy experienced the world-spirit as the essence of reason in man, *anthropos*. This experience expressed itself, in a political sense, through the development of a form of democracy that attempted to establish political rights and duties by means of the "word" by free discussion. The electorate was to be persuaded by a more or less inspired rhetoric. No longer were there divinely guided law-givers as in earlier times; cosmic reason, the *nous*, was now to speak through all free men. But this exposed man to temptation through the demagogical misuse of rhetoric. Indeed, democracy grew up in close proximity to demagogy.

With the advent of Christianity, a profound inner change occurred. The further progress of democracy cannot be understood unless we grasp the nature of Christianity as historical fact, prepared and brought about by the spirit. It may fairly be said that democracy must be Christianity made real in the realm of rights.

The influence of Christianity wrought such a change in social relations that slavery faded out. In principle, every person was regarded as an immortal soul, entitled, despite individual imperfections, to all the rights of a member of the human community. Even Augustine's doctrine of predestination could not alter this. The distinction could no longer be maintained between those who only heard the voice of reason and those who possessed it. And it was nothing but this change of consciousness and this new world conception that caused all persons to be drawn into the political community. Through this feeling for an equality of spiritual origin, the soul of man was prepared to bring forth a new social organization.

The medieval political structure of ranks and orders, based on the inequality of lord and vassal, faded away in its turn. For hundreds of years, this feudal system, although necessary, had a hampering effect on the unfolding democratic impulse, but in modern times it could no longer determine the political forms of changing Western man.

Under the influence of Christianity, the supersensible world reason, *nous*, took form among men as the philosophy and science of the Middle Ages. At the beginning of modern times this kind of thinking veered portentously. It renounced the spiritual world. The old spiritual view of the world changed into its opposite; it became materialistic. In the 17th century, Bacon severed the lower intellect from the higher reason. The latter he left to speculative philosophy, on which he set little value. He asserted that the intellect, applied inductively to sense observations, was the only reliable means of attaining knowledge. Modern materialistic science was born. This science in turn, which denied that the spirit existed or could be known, produced the technology on which our industrial economy is based. Theoretical science was supported and influenced by the philosophies of Locke, Hume, Kant and the agnostic doctrines of Mill and Spencer, etc. The evolution of science and philosophy toward the famous *"Ignorabimus"* runs parallel with the gestation of *Homo Oeconomicus*, who came to birth in the 19th century under the aegis of materialistic interpretations of history.

It is easy to see the social consequences of yet another change of consciousness—which may be called a deviation towards nihilism. A transvaluation of all values into the value of money took place. Even men could be bought and sold. Not their bodies, as in the time of slavery, but their whole lives, through the ability to deal with their "labor-power" as a commodity on the "labor market." The body was protected by *habeas corpus*, that fundament of democratic law; but all knowledge of the reality of soul and spirit was lost. Human consciousness had lost the vision of the spirit as a sphere of immediate, apprehensible reality, now contracted to an invisible point.

Yet this point, as the human ego, made itself felt with the irresistible life-force of an acorn buried beneath a tombstone. From the very beginning of the new age, however, this ego of modern man has been exposed to doubt of its own Cartesian reality. And under the influence of scientific thinking, this doubt seemed to harden into the conviction that the ego was devoid of spirit. The ego's connection with the spiritual world had been obscured.

But democracy had to develop within the generally accepted thought-life. For the proletarian, it lay buried in the grave of a materialistic conception of history; for the man of wealth, it lay in the grave of a materialistic way of living. It still lies there, awaiting resurrection.

If we are to awaken the democratic impulse, we must become aware how modern man instinctively draws out of the ego-experience increasing strength to feel himself as a single personality, confronting the world from within the physical body.

The growth of certain aspects of the democratic impulse was hastened by the awakening consciousness of personality. In the 17th century, as parliamentarianism, democracy prepared for its great expansion. The growing power of England paved the way, as the power of Rome had done for the external spread of Christianity. The French and (North) American Revolutions were the most important milestones on its road toward worldwide significance. The growth was rapid during the 19th century, although Germany, the intermediary between East and West,[86] had failed to support the Frankfurt Parliament in 1848, and thus had foregone the possibility of developing a democracy based on the spirit, turning instead to a materialistic form of the democratic idea.

However, the triumphal progress did not embrace the rest of Europe. Russia remained outside its orbit, although Peter the Great, by introducing modern techniques into social life, had begun the Europeanization of his country. Moreover, the peace of Nystadt in 1721 had brought Russia, as a spiritual, political and economic power into closer relationship with Europe. Shortly after this, with the peace of Paris in 1763, the North American colonies, a breeding ground for democracy of the Western type, came into more active relation with

---

86 The image of Germany as the middle needs elaboration and
     clarification. Especially today, what are we to understand by it? —ED.

Europe.[87] Thus the ground was prepared for the industrialization of all mankind. Both democracy and its Russian antithesis became vehicles of industrialization.

In the 20th century prior to the First World War, parliamentarianism was already approaching its fall. The absolutists gained in power. It is tragic to see how, in the First World War, the military victory of the nations representing the "true" democracy only ushered in the collapse of the democratic idea. The personal defeat of Wilson in his own country is an outer symbol of this event. The costlier victory in the Second World War, which was fought in alliance with undemocratic Russia, seems to complete this defeat. The 1941 Atlantic Charter of Roosevelt and Churchill died soon after its birth.[88] The United Nations is increasingly felt to be a mere ghost, neither loved nor feared. Democracy cannot thrive among these phantoms. It needs the sunlight of knowledge to illuminate its genuine human essence, the water of moral imagination and the fertile soil of good will. Is it not possible that the cause of the collapse is that the democratic impulse, during and even before its period of triumph, became sullied by an admixture of opposing elements that contained tendencies contrary to its own nature? Tendencies of this kind were bound to falsify democracy and eventually destroy it.

We should not fail to mention that the deeper impulses at work among the Swiss have heretofore protected them

---

87   See Rudolf Steiner, *The Art of Lecturing,* Oct. 11–16, 1921 (CW 339), Mercury Press, Spring Valley, NY, 1994.

88   For a detailed account of how this came about, see the first-hand account, H.V. Morton, *Atlantic Meeting*, Methuen, London, 1943. Morton was a well-known journalist and travel writer. The book is prefaced by Henry Longfellow's "Sail on O ship of state / Sail on, O union strong and great! Humanity with all its fears / With all the hopes of future years / Is hanging breathless on thy fate!"

from exposing their democracy to destructive forces in the same degree as other nations. Erich Kahler, in his valuable book *Man the Measure*,[89] has pointed to the purer form of democratic life in Switzerland. He stresses that in the Swiss communities, as in other parts of Europe, Christianity had dissolved the core of pagan tribal coherence, yet there remained the original communal form, with equality in feelings and customs among the members. He remarks: "Thus what remained appeared as true democracy."

Without Blood or Egotism

The struggle for democracy is in itself an historical proof that Western man has stripped off the collective feeling of tribe, race and nation given by a common blood. The collective feeling, manifesting itself spiritually through a common folk-consciousness, belongs to the past. It represents a form of community life that was spiritual, but also dependent upon the individual's lack of freedom.

The metamorphosis of the dream-like collective consciousness into individual consciousness gave rise to modern democracy as a legal order. Through it, the single person gains more significance within the group. Had democracy evolved in a straight line it would have become the sort of community life that is based on the spirit, but born out of individual freedom. It would have rested, not on a collective consciousness, but on the individual experience of man's common descent from the Universal Spirit of Mankind. Christ's words about the "Son of Man" imply an ego-experience that can be attained by modern man, but only independently of

---

89 Op. cit. Another reference could well be *The Federalist Attitude*, op. cit. —ED.

the bloodstream. Its significance for present and future social life must be appreciated. Out of this experience there can grow true democracy. Likewise, an inner vision of the true idea of democracy, namely the idea of equality, may lead to the same experience. It attests the spiritual fact of the immortality of the individual.

However, what had been experienced since the Middle Ages was not the immortal individuality but its temporal expression, the particular personality. This is only a single appearance of the individual being. When reincarnated under different conditions, the individuality takes on a new form and thus the garment of a new personality.

Bacon fettered science to sense-observation and the mortal in nature. Inspired by the same spirit, Shakespeare bound artistic vision to the many-hued but mortal personality.[90] The spirit of Hamlet's father shows itself not as an individuality but as a ghost. Hamlet himself cannot believe

---

90 CHB: One might bridle at this remark about Shakespeare, disappointed that one cannot interrogate Behrens about it. Richard Ramsbotham, the author of *Who wrote Bacon?*, in which he explores the statements of Rudolf Steiner that "the same spirit" was King James VI (I), commented: "Not quite sure what to say about it; in fact Behrens's words themselves seem to try and bind such a mighty spirit into too small a frame." What occurs to me in all this, and especially the link of the English (Anglo-Saxon, Anglo-American) to economic materialism, is that, when we arrive at a godless world, as we must, if at that point we, the English, do not see and advocate a spiritual world of the kind known to anthroposophy, *via the medium of financing the initiatives of I-beings*, everything will fall into the domain of the commodity. We have in that way, through finance, to reverse our denial of the spirit. This cannot be done to us, neither by cultures outside us, nor by regulations self-imposed; it has to be done to us by us. For example, as lenders who demand no collateral, or borrowers who refuse to give any. Out of our own understanding, i.e., recognition of the I in oneself or in others, and so through our own deeds, we must inhabit, as it were, and give life to what Steiner calls "personal credit."

in the immortal individual. The sight of a fresh grave and a weathered skull leads him to sigh in despair that the flesh of Alexander, now changed to dust, might serve to stop a bung-hole. He further says:

> Imperious Caesar, dead and turn'd to clay,
> Might stop a hole to keep the wind away.
> O, that that Earth, which kept the world in awe,
> Should patch a wall to expel the winter's flaw.

Yet, strangely enough, Hamlet's own figure, his personality with its individual destiny, stimulates us to search for the immortal individuality behind the transient form. The awakening of the personality-experience was not recognized as the door to the world of individuality. On the contrary, *it* was taken as the point of departure for all thinking, feeling, and willing. Therefore, it could lead only to egoism.

In this connection, let us take note of a curious passage in *The New Atlantis,* Bacon's Utopian description of an ideal state inspired by the scientific spirit and governed by scientists. The narrator closes his tale with the hint that he received a large farewell gift of money. Mammon seems to have had the last word. Mephisto pops out of the trapdoor. In view of this *entirely uncalled-for* mention of money, we cannot help but feel a mysterious connection with that flaw of character that later led Bacon, when Lord Chancellor, to be impeached for taking bribes.

As a "personality," the democratic man wished to protect one's personal interests by having a voice in legal and rights matters. The democratic movement began to be governed more by egoism than by the essential democratic impulse. When entangled in egoism and unable to press forward to the individuality, the personality can never allow others the same rights that it claims for itself. It seeks always for superior rights, even if this throws heavier burdens upon others. Egoism can preach the ideal of equal rights and can even give it a logical foundation, as in the doctrine of natural law. But it can never practice it. The ideal of equality becomes a mere phrase. Egoism as it works in economic life and in power-politics must either be held in check by true democracy or be transformed by a spiritual life made independent of government and the economy. Otherwise it must necessarily destroy democracy and the whole social organism. The process of destruction gains in power and speed as the single egoists, out of the same selfish interests, band together into groups. The democratic idea, which represents a profoundly moral intuition, can only be realized through moral imagination.

As the perception of the personality should be the door to the conscious experience of the awakened individuality, so the individuality has the task of overcoming egoism and thereby gaining in strength. As men become aware of the individuality and slowly bring it to birth, the path is cleared for democracy to grow strong and move ahead. Liberals speak much of progress, but it will occur only under these conditions.

Then the desire will awaken in men to assume duties voluntarily and to execute them in an individual manner for the benefit of the whole community. Through free moral intuition *they* will be able to see what is needed. This will even be easier if external conditions are difficult and chaotic, for the necessities of the situation are then more apparent. Moral imagination, arising out of intuition, will be required in order to solve the problems of life in a practical way. The moral technique of action will have a healing effect.

The proponent of such an ethical individualism[91] need not worry about establishing his own rights. Such rights will be set up in the democratic way, i.e., through the moral judgment of the majority. Only through recognition and realization of social ideas through "ethical individualism" can the citizens of the few remaining democracies avoid the threatened loss of their rights and give these ideas an impulse that conforms to the needs of our modern age. Thoughts as motives of social actions are not "categorical imperatives" that drop down from unfathomable realms as fixed ideas and suggest to the soul the duty of obeying an enigmatic moral world-law. The fettering law is replaced by the action fulfilled in love and becoming free by means of this love. Men will desire to realize the *idea* of action, which has been grasped in its lawful connection with the whole world of ideas.

Materialistic collectivism considers freedom as a pernicious delusion and wants to destroy it. Egoism wants to use freedom in an anti-social way. Both combine to destroy true democracy, which rests on a knowledge of the idea of man and on the effort to realize this idea within the rights life of human society. Egoism conceals the light of this idea; collectivism darkens it. Both produce a pseudo-democracy, which is only a prelude to the seizure of power by despotism.

We must mention another alien by-product of the evolution of democracy during the last few centuries. This is the materialistic world-conception, the true source of collectivism. Whereas the egoist overvalues his own personality, the scientific materialist undervalues the true nature of all men. The materialist regards man as an animal, bred up to his

---

91 Of the kind described in Rudolf Steiner's book, *The Philosophy of Freedom,* op. cit.

present state by the mechanistic struggle for existence. When the materialistic mode of thinking is applied to the social organism, it tries to shape it not after the living image of the true human being, but after the shadowy phantom of a mechanistic universe that is mathematically calculable. De La Mettrie spoke of "Man, the Machine." Now we have "Society, the Machine," in which mankind is no longer a living whole, but only the dead part of a dead whole. The unique personality loses all social value, while the individuality, the pure essence of the Indivisible, is regarded as theoretically unreal and practically impermissible.

Under the spell of this way of thinking, the "practical people" must laugh at a truly modern man like the poet, Christian Morgenstern, who wrote in his diary on August 7th, 1908: "I have just read Schleiermacher's assertion that the whole universe, the divine, lives in every individuality. Is this not my own thought? Have I ever known Schleiermacher before?" As a matter of fact, it *was* his own thought, for when he was 23, he wrote: "I would not care to live if my ego did not live." And later on, in 1907: "I also once believed in the greatness of technology, but now I only feel that it is taking the magic from the earth by vulgarizing everything for everybody."[92]

As one consequence for the mechanistic world-conception, the individuality with its creative forces is unavoidably excluded from social life. This world-conception that, as offspring of modern science, could only have been born under the liberal conditions offered by democracy, despoils this democracy of the true essence of its life-forces. Without these life-forces, it cannot develop further in conformity

---

92 See *The Philosophy of Freedom*, op. cit.

with reality. The exclusion of the individuality is accomplished, among other ways, by commercializing individual talents or prostituting them to nationalism or collectivism. When this exclusion is combined with personal egoism, there arises what we in the United States call the political machine. He senses that this machine, as the tool of parties or pressure-groups in capturing votes, is the greatest enemy of the genuine democratic ideal. But he feels himself powerless against it.

Democracy has become externalized and frail through being mixed with corrupt spiritual impulses and misunderstood economic interests. But democracy can be purified and brought back to life if the personality awakens to the individuality.

Democracy . . . One Day

The democratic impulse is not yet at the end of its influence. Its institutional forms and traditional methods are old and weak, but the impulse itself is still youthful. However, if it is to play a vigorous part in the future, every man must strive to create in his own soul the conditions for understanding and experiencing its true nature. Only thus can we create the external conditions for organizing it in such a way that it can become the expression of modern political life. This could assure the peace that all men long for. They will then become aware that the individual human rights that they demand for themselves must also be allowed to all their fellows. Examples of such rights are: protection from economic exploitation of "labor-power" and intelligence—i.e., a proper share of the total labor product; security in childhood, old age, and illness; freedom to develop and apply personal capacities and to participate in scientific, artistic, and religious life; the right to join with others to cultivate common interests; and a voice in the adoption of constitutions and laws.

The justified demand for human rights can only be fulfilled if the political life is treated as a special field of the social organism, in which the controlling factor is the individual interest in equal democratic rights for all. This interest in our fellow men is not simply a gift of nature. It must be brought to consciousness and cultivated by the soul. Its highest form is the recognition that each man is connected with his fellows by destiny. This is the law of karma.[93]

All the members of a people share a common destiny. This is equality through community. When we become aware that we share our destinies with our contemporaries, we are led to experience equality within a wider karmic sphere, namely in regard to the *Zeitgeist* or spirit of the age. If, going further, we attain to a feeling of common karmic relationships with the dead and the unborn, we reach a brotherly concord with the Spirit who, as a Cosmic Being, has linked Himself with the destiny of the earth and of mankind. The rights life, taken in its profoundest sense, must receive its impulses from the order of karmic relationships, consciously experienced through spiritual-scientific methods. Otherwise we shall have no order of human rights, but only an order of human wrongs.

Thus, democracy expresses more and more the individuality's endeavor justly to organize that domain of human relationships which demands the establishment and development of man's rights. This domain must be separated

---

93 See Rudolf Steiner, *An Outline of Occult Science,* CW 13.

from the other spheres of interest. It must be organized on its own foundation, so as to function in organic relation to the other spheres. But two other spheres need be considered: *spiritual life* and the *domain of economy*. The social organism is *threefold*.

Since the beginning of modern times, the economic and spiritual realms, like the political, have struggled to establish themselves on a universal basis. Should this urge come to expression without providing each of these domains with its own organization, then the inorganic medley of the three would bring about on a worldwide basis the same mutual destruction as now takes place within national boundaries. Selfish economic interests would corrupt the political and spiritual realms. One-sided scientific and religious doctrines, becoming fanatical, would drive politics as well as economics in the wrong direction. National and other groups, lusting for political power, would interfere with economic and spiritual life. Error and evil, as well as truth and goodness, are universal forces. They work in the same way in the universal as in the national realm and with immeasurably increased catastrophic power. A super-national,[94] monolithic state, a world-government, would negate true internationalism and extend the defects of the single states to the whole globe. Sponsors of such a state forget that civil wars are always the bloodiest, and that a world civil war would by no means be impossible. True democracy could not live within such a monolithic world-state. On the other hand, the whole social organism will flourish when people will have grasped the

---

94   As noted in our introduction, we have been careful when using "super-national." Often, Behrens uses the term "supra-national," but, to avoid serious confusion, we have replaced that with "universal." —ED.

idea of the threefold social organism. Then, as national and other groups and in accordance with the individual abilities of their members, they will develop suitable rights, spiritual and economic institutions under separate administrations. The universal interrelation of these three spheres of interests and functions will have to be based on the universal evolution independently undergone by each separate sphere.

Rudolf Steiner wrote in great detail about the social problems of our time and outlined the threefolding of society as a challenge to modern consciousness to find the only solution that would bring it a living impulse for its eventual salvation. This important historic impulse has been stressed here from the viewpoint of democracy's presently endangered position.

We can now answer our opening question about the character of a new consciousness. The democratic movement sprang out of the transformation of the old collective consciousness into individual consciousness. We have hardly begun to tap the spiritual potentialities of this new consciousness. They have been obscured by the many-sided egoistic aims of the personality and by the consequences of a one-sided materialistic world-conception. If a sufficient number of people can overcome their personal egoism and surmount this scientific error about the nature of the world, then individual consciousness will be able to create a threefold social order out of its own being.

In this threefold order, democratic laws, based on the idea of equality, will keep economic interests within bounds and provide spiritual aspirations with the needed living space to unfold in freedom and thus endow man's existence with a loftier meaning. When this has been accomplished on a worldwide basis, which protects each nation's cultural tasks without encroaching upon its national production and consumption of goods, democracy will be reborn. The moment at which this rebirth will take place depends on the living comprehension of the threefold order idea and the vigor of will-power devoted to its realization.

9

The Economic Essentials
of the Cultural Life

The source of true culture is not to be found in the domain of economy. No interplay of economic forces can engender science, art or religious life. Culture, the expression of man's spiritual existence, does not spring from the sphere of economy. The essential function of economy is to care for bodily needs—in other words, to provide for man's material existence.[95]

Nor is the state the source of spiritual life. The state is an expression of the fact that, as a result of given conditions, men feel themselves as belonging to a certain group, and consequently wish to order their intercourse on the basis of a shared rights life. Economic activity and the rights life are social realms that must be differentiated from the purely spiritual realm. Our cultural impulses—for example, the vitalization and cultivation of the feeling for right, the development of economically productive capacities, and self-control in determining economic needs—arise from another source.

The true source of culture is neither an abstract concept nor the result of lucky chance. Spiritual man himself brings

95 CHB: Only by serving as a field for giving expression to one's capacities!

forth culture as something essentially creative in earthly life—proof of his free relationship to a universal spiritual world. The heartbeat of culture is experienced in art; its head is seen in the scientific life; its healing hand is felt in moral-religious activity.[96]

Culture has its source in that realm to which man, as a free spirit, has acquired access through self-mastery, and in which he enters into relationship with other free spirits.[97] Only when, as a spiritual being urged toward development and led by a sense of truth, he studies life's enigmas, does science come into being. Through culture, truth becomes the torch of scientific life. Art emerges[98] only when man, in free creation, reveals hidden truth by transforming the matter and forces provided by nature into human creations that transcend nature. Through art the cosmic harmony inherent in beauty becomes the shaping life element in cultural existence, overcoming all discord. As for religion, it becomes a social reality when the individual embodies, in action and attitude, what has been inwardly experienced in cognition and externally revealed in art. Through religion the good becomes a human-social fact, and thereby the vital content of culture.

Although the realms of economy and rights cannot of themselves produce cultural impulses, yet, for this very reason—and in accordance with their own peculiar features—they must be brought into intelligent relationship with the

---

96 Later, Behrens links science to education, art to healing, and religion to redemption. —ED.

97 CHB: Would it not be better to speak of self-discovery leading to the possibility of self-development and self-mastery?

98 The reference seems to be to visual, physical art, rather than literature, for example. —ED.

spiritual sphere proper. This can be achieved only by one whose life is shaped by his participation in all three regions of social existence. Upon an ordered economy within the body social, the spiritual life arising from the individual spirit is borne through *time;* whereas the rights life clears the *space* in which the spirit of true culture can unfold in accordance with its own being—that is, in freedom.

This treatise has set for its aim a clarification of the relationship between economy and a free spiritual life, and the task of the political life will be given only as much consideration as seems necessary to achieve this end. From the presentation of these basic interrelationships, we will arrive at an insight into those forces of impetus and of resistance that prevent such temporal and spatial shaping of vital conditions as is demanded by the ideal nature of the social organism itself. These forces have broken up the venerable relation of human society to matter and to spirit. They have driven social forms and conditions into chaos; and out of disintegrated matter and anarchistic forces they have contrived with superhuman lawlessness to construct a spiritless, sub-human domain fueled like a gigantic machine with the degraded will-substance of mankind. In this domain, there is no *Lebensraum* left for man as a free spirit, but only a field of death upon which he continues to function mechanically, like a robot in the service of a universal destructive force. Control and transformation of this force will be brought about by cognition of good and evil. Only a timely perception of the manner in which good and evil work in our present epoch can show us how to found the culture of the future.

The Cultural Aspect Of Money

By studying the manner in which men of today spend their earnings, insight can be gained into the relation between economic and spiritual life. In order to clarify what follows it should be pointed out that the concept *earned income*[99] is one that has had scientific significance only for about 300 years—that is, since the division of labor became the basic principle of modern economy.[100] The concept cannot be applied to the more or less patriarchal economic forms of earlier times. There was then, naturally, no question of compensation for work in the form of money, for in ancient civilizations the burden of economic production rested principally upon the shoulders of slaves, serfs, bondsmen and the like, not to mention the work performed by women. Many remnants of the patriarchal economic system, rooted in agriculture, persisted into the 19th century and can still be studied in the tradition-bound East as evidence of the original form of economy.

By reason of the manner in which modern man takes part in production and consumption, he is compelled to spend his earned income, putting money back into circulation. But few people realize that there are sharply differentiated channels through which spent money flows back into circulation.

One portion of a person's income procures the immediate necessities of life, such as food, clothing and shelter. This part serves to maintain physical existence and flows,

---

99 Distinct from unearned income—investment dividends and the like. But see later discussion. —ED.

100 In general social-scientific discourse, "modern" history begins in 1500, a date that in anthroposophy marks the beginning of the consciousness-soul period. —ED.

per Steiner, as *purchase money* into circulation. It pays for corresponding equivalents in the form of goods or services.

A second portion of income is saved. The fact that for extensive strata of the population the earned income is too low to permit of savings will be omitted from consideration as abnormal.[101] We are speaking here of the general tendency to save, and of the fact that the saving of income has become a general economic habit. The idea is that savings shall be spent for necessities, not upon receipt, but at some later date. Meanwhile they are loaned, and thereby become *loanmoney*.[102] These flow into banks, savings banks, investment trusts, and other financial institutions. As loan-money, this portion of income finds its way into a sphere of circulation to be clearly distinguished from that of purchase-money. The investor of loan-money becomes a creditor, the recipient a debtor who uses the borrowed sum either to establish a new production branch or to extend one already in operation. Cases in which loan-money is not applied to such productive uses will here be disregarded as abnormal and, for the total economy, unimportant. Although the figure stamped upon purchase-money and upon loan-money refers to the same substance of currency (gold, silver, or some other raw material) the two money functions have in reality quite different [meanings and] values within economic circulation. Purchase-money serves as a medium of exchange and a measure

---

101 CHB: How can "extensive strata" be abnormal when it is widespread? Moreover, in a healthy economy, just as after savings come donations of surplus funds, so before savings comes disposable income, that is to say, income enough not to lead an economic life of mere subsistence.

102 CHB: Savings are money lent to banks. They equate with loan money because they are both saved and lent. In this sense, loan money refers to both sides of the balance sheet.

of value. To the buyer, <u>its worth is measured (or covered)</u>[103] by what it will buy in utility values; to the seller, by what he can sell or produce in new commodities. Loan-money, on the other hand, as a means of new capital investments, becomes bound up with the individual capacities of the borrower. It is worth as much as he can, with its help, accomplish in supplying certain economic necessities; and it must therefore be measured by an entirely different standard of value. The value of loan-money is determined by the success of the borrower's productive contribution.

There is a third way of <u>circulating</u> income that again has a different function in the social totality. This third portion of earned income serves to satisfy those cravings whose presence in everyone proves that man lives not by bread alone. Out of the depths of his innermost being the need to participate in spiritual life forces itself upward into his consciousness. He wants to educate himself, to extend his spiritual horizon by gathering and digesting the fruits of science. He wants to gain access to the life of art, and to have the spirit manifested in the beautiful embodiment of architecture, sculpture, music, painting, poetry and the art of movement. And through devotion to religious impulses, he seeks to experience, consciously, the intimate bond between his true being and the Being of the World. <u>This money circulates as grants and donations.</u>[104]

Here we encounter the real, the pure spiritual needs of man. Under the conditions imposed by modern forms of

---

103 The underlined passages below are rewordings of Behrens's formulations to make them comprehensible in terms of both Rudolf Steiner's concepts and those of conventional economics. —ED.

104 Transfers of excess wealth from the point of view of the transferor. —ED.

economy and politics, these spiritual needs have the peculiar function of determining, in a way, the trend of culture, through this third way of <u>circulating</u> income. The money is not employed for buying goods: one cannot buy a sermon or participation in a religious ceremony, nor does one really buy anything when admitted to a theatrical performance or to a scientific lecture. This only appears so on the surface; and the illusion is accepted as truth because consciousness is obscured by a one-sided, commercialistic imagination that sees all values as commodities and mentally converts them into money values.

In reality, buying and selling take place only in the realm where commodities and consumption services are exchanged. There, economic values are exchanged for economic equivalents. "Products" of the spirit, on the other hand, cannot be "consumed" in the economic sense. Consumption implies destruction, and purely cultural achievements are not destroyed by being received; that is, they do not depreciate. On the contrary, their receipt enhances their social value. Such results of the scientific, the artistic and the religious life are experienced, and they live on in the souls of those who receive and transmute them. The scientist, the artist and the priest perform no economic labor, either in connection with the means of production or upon the soil. On the contrary, it is a condition of their purely cultural work that they be relieved of the necessity of performing economic, i.e., physical, labor. They are thus relieved by receiving gifts; and everyone who spends money for the satisfaction of cultural needs should know that in reality he is only <u>transferring</u> such money <u>to others to spend, save (i.e., lend) or give</u>. The donor relieves the exponents of the spiritual life of economic work in proportion to the amount given, which represents the equivalent of economic work on the part of the donor. Thus, for example, the payment of the price of a theater ticket is not a purchase but a portion of the total sum donated to the maintenance of a certain artistic enterprise. The advice of a physician or of a lawyer is a purely spiritual contribution, not exchangeable for an economic commodity, but rather made possible by the donation of the equivalent of the latter. A clergyman is relieved of economic labor by his congregation so that he may satisfy an inner craving of its members.[105] For this the congregation makes sacrifices. Thus, to the function of purchase-money and *loan-money* must be added that of *gift-money*.[106]

The concept of gift-money is an indispensable one in a realistic social and economic science. It is demanded by the facts; and it establishes another equally important concept: that of *non-compensatory income*.[107] Activity within the purely spiritual realm is not labor in the economic sense. The ingrained habit of coloring the concept "labor" with a moral tinge destroys its scientific applicability. Its use should be limited to the activity called for in economic production. Only in this way can labor performed in the production of

---

105 Craving in connection with spiritual life sounds a little strange, but we have left it alone. —ED.

106 BB: In his series of lectures entitled *Economics*, Rudolf Steiner deals with the money problem, among others. He shows that a realistic science of economics cannot do without the knowledge that the function of money is threefold. Only a practical application of the scientific concepts "purchase money," "loan money" and "gift money" can harmonize the amount of money and the rate at which it circulates, as well as its use, with the exigencies of the social organism. The present treatise also attempts to show how such concepts can be fruitful in solving not only economic but general sociological problems as well.

107 Changed from "unearned income." —ED.

goods intended for consumption be clearly differentiated from creative activity producing purely cultural values in the spiritual life. Such a distinction is essential if one would arrive at clear and living ideas that can be a constructive force in the social life.[108]

The possibility for spiritual creation to come into being out of full individual freedom, and to expand unhindered in the social field, presupposes the intention, on the part of those interested in true culture, to grant the representatives of spiritual initiative an income that does not represent a return for corresponding economic labor. In this sense, and in no other, can such an income be designated "non-compensatory." As concerns the goods produced within economy itself, exponents of spiritual life are in a sense *pure consumers*.[109]

---

108 CHB: It is surely contentious that actors do not labor, only the makers of things. In economics, "labor" includes manual and mental activity (indeed, the one can hardly be separated from the other). Work on nature and work on one's skills (both also forms of working on oneself) are a more concrete, albeit also complex, way of describing the economics of being a preacher. Indeed, the idea that a vicar is financed by his or her congregation is today a concept that is generally both quaint and anachronistic. It serves well as Steiner's illustration of the relationship between the peasants in an agrarian village and their priest—but it hardly cuts ice in today's Paul Samuelson world.

109 BB: Karl Marx's materialistic conception of history sees purely spiritual activity as only ideology, and for a materialistic socialist, ideology has no reality. For him, only that economy is real that has its origin in man's material necessities and their satisfaction. The only salvation is seen in socializing the means of production, the legal duty of participation by all in production work, and equitable distribution of products. Away with unearned income acquired by non-workers through the exploitation of workers! The concept unearned income is employed by Marxism to characterize the propertied class that consumes the surplus values of which the unendowed working class is deprived. This concept is obscured by the resentment of a certain class that is in conflict with another. It has become entangled with moral considerations. What we are here endeavoring to show, however, is the fact that a genuine science of

Another view of the problem indicated by our title opens up when we recognize the fact that within social life the existence of such pure consumers is justified, because without them the social organism would be doomed to spiritual death. Science, art and religion—the true, the beautiful and the good—come to practical expression in the social realm as education, healing, and redemption. Everything connected with instruction, with the cultivation of human aptitudes and with the perfecting of the individual human being, can bear fruit only through a sound collaboration between the cognition of truth, the manifestation of art, and the experience of moral intuitions. This is the realm in which the younger generation is educated. Only within the frame of a free spiritual life can members of the younger generation be given a true general education. Only thus can their moral stamina and technical talents be aroused and developed in a manner enabling them later on to achieve results in the economic and political life, such as the future has a right to expect of them; or in the realm of culture itself, should this be their calling.[110]

Now, for as long as a child attends school and until he has completed his advanced studies, he works only at himself. He performs no productive economic work. Therefore,

---

economy and sociology must recognize the necessity of incomes not earned by working within the field of goods production. Precisely by creating the conditions under which everyone can admit the justification (instead) for non-compensatory incomes, the conditions are at the same time created for the elimination of unjustifiable ones. In this the aim cannot be to satisfy some moral demand, but to accord spiritual life its economic base. The degree to which moral demands are also then satisfied will depend upon the efficacy of the social impulses emanating from spiritual life.

110 CHB: Again, the nuance that spiritual life has a higher or special status, as if only some people belong or exist there.

he must be provided with the economic necessities, and he is another case of "pure consumer." From this viewpoint, it is wholly immaterial whether the child or youth derives his subsistence from home, from a private or public institution, or from any other source. In any case, that portion of the social product devoted to the younger generation represents non-compensatory income that can be expressed in terms of money. It is a donated income; and because, in the present condition of economy, donations are as a rule made in money—or at least can always be calculated in terms of money—they constitute gift-money.[111] From time immemorial, the economic instinct to provide for the maintenance, education and spiritual fostering of the coming generation has had its source in the deepest moral impulses of working mankind, and this is still the case today.

Out of the same depths of the human soul whence flow the impulses to work for those not yet able to work, there arises the impulse to support those no longer able to work, to render their declining years free from economic anxieties. Thus, the material existence of the older generation also depends upon non-compensatory income, upon the functioning of gift-money. A person too old to work is again a pure consumer; and both the young and the old generations are essentially connected with the spiritual life, though in different ways. The young, as bearers of the future, are brought up by the present generation within the framework of spiritual life. Their soul-spiritual forces of growth are brought to

---

111 CHB: Behrens surely means donations and only if they are truly given, in effect converting loan money into purchase money. This is a topic that brings with it a major cousin-topic, aging and dying money, that Behrens, interestingly, makes no mention of. This would hardly include, for example, today's money market making student loans.

blossom. The old, as representatives of the past, have experience of life; they can advise the present generation. The task of teaching the young and forming their character releases creative impulses within spiritual life. The necessity of coping with life's problems should awaken in the intermediate generation an inclination to seek advice from their elders. In this way, the old, too, enjoy a fundamental, purely soul-spiritual relation to social existence. The old are not dross carried along in the stream of social life, but rather, an essential factor of that life, side by side with the other two: those at the height of their activity and the young. Parenthetically, recall what the "Assembly of Old Men" meant in ancient cultures. The word "senate" derives from the Latin *senex,* meaning old man: the word "old" connoted wisdom as well as age. It is a sign of our own time that "old" no longer means "wise"; and this points to something that must be re-acquired upon a new plane of consciousness. The lack of wisdom in the old of today, their helpless attitude toward the world situation, and their inability to give any worthy advice—all this is proof of impotence in a spiritual life corrupted by political and economic interests.[112]

A third category of pure consumers is comprised of those who must be cared for as a result of illness or physical impairments that prevent them from working. For the duration of their inability to work, these, too, enjoy non-compensatory income. The presence of this group of pure consumers tends

---

112 CHB: Behrens paints an important, if evocative, picture of a society in which being active and being able to work (i.e., labor in its twofold sense) is the essence of being human. How different to a world in which many seek their income, not from recognition of their work done for others, but avoiding work by playing the real estate and stock markets, looking to their inheritance or lottery-gambling.

to awaken those deep and spiritual social impulses that have to do with healing.[113] A true spiritual life would be unthinkable without the will to explore the forces of healing and to raise them to social efficacy. Just as life is not a static condition, but a dynamic development from birth to death, requiring the passage through death to attain to new birth, so health is not a static condition, but a matter of dynamic balance that must ever be re-achieved, confronted as it is by health destroying powers. The life of the social organism needs death in order to unfold again in ever-higher forms. Health needs sickness in order to re-appear upon ever higher planes of existence as self-achieved harmony with the infinite. This profound connection between death and life, sickness and health, is divined by those to whom healing means more than the external restoration of interrupted working capacity in the (narrow) economic sense.

We have endeavored to endow the concept "culture" with a content capable of providing an insight into the economic conditions indispensable to the establishment, maintenance, and development of a genuine culture. The material existence of a free spiritual life can be justified and informed with a higher purpose only through the sacrifices brought to it in the right spirit by men working at agriculture or industrial production, as also in service "industries." These sacrifices[114] can only be such as the individual makes in consequence of individual standards of value. A free spiritual life should not be sustained by state-levied taxes. Such taxes

---

113 This should be extended to include mental illnesses and that most profound case if "pure consumption" combined with deep karma, those with so-called "social needs." —ED.

114 CHB: Sacrifices only in the sense of footnote 42—that is, transfers of excess, non-needed wealth from one party to another.

would represent imposed sacrifices, hence be no sacrifices at all. That is the method of financing the spiritual life without reference to a sense of individual sacrifice, and it is the surest way to destroy freedom of the spirit.

The social life presents still another feature that today vividly emphasizes the pregnancy of such concepts as "pure consumption," "non-compensatory income" and "gift-money," as well as the indisputable need of realizing them in full consciousness. We refer to the fact that since the advent of the technical age industrialism has become the dominating economic form. Machinery has conquered the economy and brought it completely under control. Furthermore, machinery has led to a social structure that confronts man today with weighty rights problems resulting from a juristic concept of property born of quite other conditions, but not changed by time. From the standpoint taken here, however, neither of the conditions just mentioned represents the full determining significance of the machine in shaping society: it is the essential relationship of the economically active human being to the spiritual life, the source of culture, which we are here considering; and from this point of view it is of fateful import that the machine saves (by extending or multiplying) economic labor. It releases man from a method of production that in former times was closely linked with nature. Through its agency, he has become independent of daylight, of the seasons, of climatic conditions, of the nature-given quality of raw materials, even of time and space; but chiefly of the quantum of available manpower needed to cover a given volume of necessities. What the economic worker does for spiritual life by sacrificing part of his income—that is, sustaining the spiritually creative pure consumer in order that he may fulfill his social and evolutionary task—the machine, in combination with economic organization, does for this worker himself. It saves him work. The amount of time and labor demanded of him is reduced, obviated.[115]

Considered in the light of historical development, these facts express themselves in a reduction in the need for heavy work, as well as in a growing tendency to reduce working hours by law. Leisure time increases. As a concomitant, we find a growing will to make man a consumer of machine products through constant improvement in labor-saving processes of production. The old curse "In the sweat of thy brow shalt thou eat bread" will soon have lost its meaning. On his path through the metamorphosis of economic forms, man tends ever more markedly toward pure consumership that receives non-compensatory income or gift-money.[116]

But in proportion as leisure increases, the problem of employing it intelligently becomes more insistent. Leisure exposes the spiritual problem in all its nakedness and reveals its significance for the present and the future. A solution to this problem can be expected only if men will spiritually transform those forces that the machine saves them in labor,

---

115 CHB: Again, Behrens's consistent division of people into latter-day classes or castes is both misleading and damaging. It is *overall* that labor (of whatever kind) expended results in labor obviated.

116 CHB: Even if it is conceivable, surely a world without people producing is unwelcome? The combined effect of division of labor and technology is not meant to be leisure in the sense of disporting oneself semi-permanently, but the doing of what Aristotle calls "fine actions." Keynes (whose work Behrens makes no reference to) is very precise in this regard—see his 1930 *Economic possibilities for our grandchildren* (in: J. M. Keynes (1963) *Essays in Persuasion*, London: Macmillan, pp. 358–374) and commentary on Aristotle by Keynes's biographer, Robert Skidelsky. Indeed, Keynes, who died in April 1946, is in many ways the bridge between Steiner and modern economics. As Stephen Vallus implies in his review, not to use this bridge weakens the practicability of Behrens's own work.

and direct them toward creative participation in spiritual life proper. No one is limited any longer to a mere interest in the fruits of spiritual research, artistic endeavor, or the religious life. Owing to the ever-decreasing expenditure of time and energy in the economic realm, it is possible for everyone to attain to creative participation in the sphere of true culture; and that is probably the most significant degree of destiny relating to modern mankind. Modern technique provides the external conditions under which the individual can enjoy economic independence; and the latter can have social meaning only through the attainment and realization of inner freedom in the realm of spiritual activity. This realization manifests itself socially as a widening and deepening of the knowledge of man and the cosmos, of the manifestation of truth through art,[117] and of the perfecting of the imperfect through religion.[118]

With the foregoing exposition, we have attempted to work out one essential feature of the relation between economic and spiritual activity. It consists of the fact that parts of the economic social product are diverted to the fostering of spiritual life. The production-surplus of one social realm, the economic life, serves as the economic foundation of another, the spiritual life. This surplus is consumed by various institutions of the spiritual life, such as schools,

---

117 Earlier Behrens linked truth to science. —ED.

118 CHB: Again, it is unfortunate that Behrens seems unaware of how in the world of conventional economics such things are known, if but little and using different language. What, for example, is the 8-hour day all about, and has been since Marx's time, but remains elusive because, of course, of the current form of capitalism and society. Behrens's critique of both would be strengthened if he evinced his participation in or at least awareness of the wider Anglo-Saxon discourse, and so helped make Rudolf Steiner's work less a stranger in regard to it.

universities, research centers, scientific institutes and expeditions, academies of art, publications, exhibitions, museums, theaters, opera houses, symphony orchestras, and the institutions of religion and of cults. This surplus, deriving from individual willingness to make sacrifices,[119] accumulates and becomes a mighty capital, *spiritual capital;* and it has this in common with capital invested in the economy: the money is linked with individual human capabilities through which it fosters the realization of ideas. But aside from this aspect, the two kinds of capital must be clearly distinguished.

Capital diverted into the spiritual sphere is completely consumed and must be continually replaced by new donations from the economy. It must not flow back into the economy, i.e., the gift-money has to be withdrawn from circulation by the banking organization in accordance with the date of expiration. Invested money, on the contrary, does return to the economy where it serves to establish, perfect, or extend economic enterprises. As has been explained, in the case of economic capital one is dealing not with the function of gift-money but of loan-money. It is inherent in loan-money that capital loaned for purposes of production is used but not used up, because it must be paid back.[120]

---

119 See footnote 41.

120 BB: Naturally, the values acquired with the original loaned capital (means of production, etc.) are also consumed—that is, worn out; they will not be merely depreciated. The valuable amount of the capital, however, remains intact, so that it can be paid back. That is the point in the present instance. The function of loaned capital is such that every money value should be bound up with the concept "depreciating value." For example, borrowed money would partially lose its value, in proportion to the period of the loan, at the moment when it is paid back to the lender. This money should either not be re-invested at all, or only for a correspondingly shorter term. In the former case, it should be employed only as purchase money to cover personal needs. Thereafter, it should be withdrawn from circulation.

Considering, further, the borrower's obligation to pay interest as compensation for the capital loan, it is clear that loan-
money functions in an entirely different rights context from
gift-money. [121]

Money thus facing depreciation could therefore best serve as gift
money—that is, for purely cultural purposes.

> We have therefore three kinds of money, qualitatively different
> from one another: purchase money, loan money, and gift
> money.... We shall find that after a certain time all that is loan
> money passes over into gift money.... Loan money must not be
> allowed to be dammed back into purchase money, for that would
> disturb the latter. Loan money, therefore, passes over into gift
> money...and what does it do in the domain where gift money
> is working? It loses its value.... It lets the purchase value vanish
> into nothing. Finally, between the two, the transition is brought
> about through loan money. The loan money itself gradually
> vanishes into gift money. (Rudolf Steiner, *Economics*, op. cit.)

A practical reform of the money system which would take
such necessities into account is a purely technical question
depending upon individual conditions prevailing in a certain area
of economic life, and presupposing the will to realize a threefold
ordering of society.

121 CHB: Here, there is the whole notion of returning capital, which
it never does. Depreciation and amortization match bookkeeping
to the reality of decay in the physical aspect of economic life,
after which the capital flows on. What is repaid to a lender is
fresh capital generated in the enterprise. But it only flows "back"
because there is a claim in it, which is an affair of rights or law,
not economics. This difference becomes obvious once "return" is
dropped from the lexicon of finance, for then what it misdescribes
will become evident. Indeed, much mischief results when matters
of right, such as interest or debt repayments falling due when
funds are not currently available, trump economic reality, forcing
the latter into a straightjacket in which the only sacrifice made
is that of entrepreneurial initiative. These concerns are being
expressed because, per Behrens's analysis, here error in economic
thinking is the cause of our economic maladies, not evil. Misplaced
opprobrium does not serve associative economics, or economics
in general, well. Tidy such matters up, however, and Behrens's
arguments will not only be strengthened, but also find their way
into channels where they are likely to get the one thing Rudolf
Steiner's work as an economist deserves but seldom enjoys: traction.

The Credit Problem and the Freedom of Cultural Life

In order to judge the function of loan-money aright one must realize that modern industrialism, with its big business and mass production, tends ever more completely to exclude financing by individuals. Industrialism has created conditions of credit that require the accumulation of enormous sums of loan-money via monetary institutions. In no other way can loan-money reach the necessary total. But this in turn means that the basis of modern industrial production is credit, and no longer—as under the former commercialist form of economy—individual private capital. Managers and executives no longer work with capital belonging to them, but with capital that others have placed at their disposal.[122]

Under these new conditions the relation between creditor and borrower has taken on a new aspect. It is no longer the rule but the exception for lender and borrower to meet for the purpose of arranging a loan on the basis of confidence arising out of an actual personal relationship. It has become necessary for the banking organization to intervene between lenders and borrowers. The banker's position toward the borrower is merely that of representative of an abstract number of unknown persons who have lent the bank moneys to be invested. The lender as an individual human being of flesh and blood has been transformed into an anonymous and shadowy collective creditor.[123]

---

122 CHB: As an example of addressing the concerns expressed in the previous footnote, this sentence could be rewritten: "Insofar as managers and executives no longer work with capital belonging to them, they work with capital which others have placed at their disposal."

123 CHB: It is precisely anonymous credit that transfers capital from ownership to usership. In anthroposophical terms, from sanguinity to the I, from Gabriel to Michael.

And the individual borrower personality is dying out as well. The vast credits that determine the fate of modern production are taken up not by single people, but by a corporation whose unknown shareholders are represented by their official plenipotentiary. Incidentally, stock shares, in spite of the difference in their legal status, are fundamentally indistinguishable from loans: basically they, too, are only loaned capital, that is, means of financing.[124] With the cessation of the meeting of the actual individuals immediately involved in the borrower-lender relationship, confidence—and credit is confidence—lost its human base.

In place of security based on confidence in the personal qualities of the borrower, the lender must put up with the risk of finding himself confronted by a Great Unknown. It is not within the scope of this treatise to enter into the problem of credit even sketchily, still less exhaustively; but what has been said about the manner in which industrial economic methods force the credit problem to the fore will serve to characterize the relation of the economic to the spiritual life from the standpoint of credit.[125]

A beginning can be made in solving the problem of credit by making up one's mind to recognize a free, independent spiritual life as a social sphere, definitely distinguished from the economic domain by its nature and its task. Confidence is an inner soul force that can be released through illusions

---

124 CHB: Not so. In principle, shares carry the risk run by the borrower who, by (debatable) convention gets the "reward" of residual value. Loans, from banks especially, are not intended for this purpose.

125 CHB: However sketchy, precisely this situation does need clarifying, if only to link it to Rudolf Steiner's treatment of the problem Behrens is referring to—financialism, the emancipation of the money markets from the goods market dating, per Steiner, from Britain's defeat of Napoleon.

as readily as through genuine cognition of truth; but the one is blind, the other seeing. While the subsequent disillusionment inevitable in the first case gradually reduces confidence to the vanishing point, the justification of confidence based upon insight raises it to an unlimited social power. To develop genuine insight into human character cannot be the province of the economic life as such, for the latter rightly deals only in production, circulation and consumption of goods; but it *is* a task of the spiritual life. Education through scientific schooling (especially in economics), artistic activity and religious awakening, self-education through self-knowledge, self-control and self-transformation—these beget a spiritual substance and cultural form from which there glows a real confidence in the spirit. And in the other realms of existence, such as economy, this confidence furthers life and establishes the feeling of security.

Granting the existence of such a spiritual life, it becomes clear that the answer to the burning question of credit, which will be decisive in shaping future economic life, must come from an entirely new and realistic direction. In this epoch of big industry and the accumulation of anonymous loaned capital, it is obvious that the credit system cannot revert to the old relationship of individual creditors and borrowers: in a sense, that has become technically impossible. But there is another way, and it is the only one that accords with reality. The disposal of (excess) loaned capital could be transferred to an institution best able to invest it wisely in economic necessities, an institution belonging to the free spiritual life and responsible only to the domain of culture. In this domain alone is to be found an informed view of the vital conditions and all interrelationships in the social organism. Here alone can an expert opinion be formed concerning the spiritual justification and justifiable satisfaction of a special economic need calling for an investment of capital. Only from the realm of free spiritual life can one judge what social changes—even revolutions—will result from a new capital investment (to exploit a new invention, for example) or how the consequences of such can best be compensated in a practical way. The reason why such a valid opinion can be formed in the free spiritual realm is because there alone exists the requisite independence from egotistical special interests, one-sided, collectivistic ideas on economic planning, political considerations, and the influence of pressure groups.[126] And finally, only the bearers of spiritual life, called to such office by virtue of character, knowledge and experience, can judge which personalities are morally and practically equipped to handle loaned capital for productive purposes. Summing up: the spiritual sphere would not function economically—that is, it would replace neither the promoter, the manager nor the bank; but it would act in an advisory capacity with legal status in matters of directing and investing capital. In this sense only would the administration of capital become a task of the spiritual sphere.

This exposition of a new credit basis would be completely misunderstood if one believed that a credit institution of this kind could have but a theoretical character, unrelated to life; and that therefore it could not prescribe decisive measures for the benefit of economic life. But spiritual life, as the term is here intended, includes not only the results of theoretical research in sociology, economics and the sciences of finance, business methods, of raw materials, technology, and so forth,

---

126 CHB: Again, why not entrust the non-egotistical entrepreneur? What else is ethical individualism in economic life?

but also the practical experience of the managers themselves, among whom the spiritual *elite* should rise to the position of teachers in their several fields within the free spiritual life.[127]

Money serving only as a measure of value and a medium of exchange circulates exclusively in the economic sphere. As loan money, it temporarily leaves this sphere, coming under the head of money justifiably placed at the disposal of the free spiritual life. There, however, it is not consumed but circulates on in the economy by way of investments—i.e., borrowers—in a wholly new form of personal credit.[128] [In this way,] gift money is entirely withdrawn from economic interests, to be completely consumed in spiritual life: economically it becomes wholly depreciated.

It would exceed the scope of this treatise to explain how these three forms of money should be integrated through a consciously directed and mathematically controlled transformation of the proper functioning of money. What we have endeavored to show is how the first fundamental relation of economic life to spiritual life—that of financial guarantor— is joined by a second: the confidence that those involved in economic life[129] can feel in the spiritual life if the first relation

---

127 CHB: If by "managers" Behrens means ethically individual entrepreneurs, okay. For then the argument is the same made by Steiner in regard to education—that only actual or experienced teachers should "manage" education. But this is true of all professions. In England, for example, this is the basis of the Royal Colleges that regularly review the evolution of their professions, updating their codes of conduct as necessary (which the rights life than adopts and enforces but does not originate). Just so, one can conceive associations (in Behrens's sense) as the province of entrepreneurs *when not acting egotistically.*

128 Presumably, this is a reference to Steiner's "personal credit"? Lending to the person, not the asset? —ED.

129 CHB: Deleted "the economic worker."

is operating effectively. Upon this confidence rests the sort of credit indispensable to modern economy.

The Spiritual Aspect of Buying

There is still a third fundamental relation between the economy and spiritual life, and it is connected with the functioning of purchase money. Like gift money and loan money, purchase money can also be considered from a purely spiritual viewpoint. In itself, purchase money is a means of circulation through which processes of production and consumption within a given area form an economic unit. Practically, purchase money as a means of payment is nothing more than legally valid evidence of economic work performed by the owner of a product, entitling him to receive a corresponding equivalent. Earned income, insofar as it comes into circulation as purchase money, serves the satisfaction of personal needs. Our relation to spiritual life becomes manifest when we observe how purchase money is spent. In this "how" is revealed the nature of the individual requirements that lead people to spend money. The total economic consumption reveals the spiritual standards of a group of people. The nature of its individual demands is like an account book, the entries in which reveal how much of a spiritual man is hidden in the economic man.[130] Such individual wants reflect our relation to spiritual life. This fact can be brought to consciousness by considering without prejudice the fundamental needs—food, clothing and shelter. If our ambition

---

130 CHB: At last! Spiritual man hidden in economic man implies that spiritual life and economic life are not separate realms. Given that, in Steiner's terms, all labor entails a mix of transforming nature (V1) and organizing labor (V2) , the conceptual difference between, say, a teacher and a road mender is the first entails more V2 than V1, the second the reverse.

stops at general physical satisfaction it lacks the spiritual element entirely and is closely related to the animal's attitude. But within modern economy the human being selects his food personally, as he does his clothing and his shelter. He determines its measure and introduces hygienic, aesthetic and moral considerations in satisfying his needs. These not only depend upon unconscious impulses, habit, customs, and tradition, but contain a consciously personal note as well. The manner in which man determines his needs is the consequence of his schooling and self-education; that is, his personal relation to spiritual life.[131]

The producer also finds in purchase money a link with spiritual life. When purchase money finally, by way of circulation, comes into the producer's hands it enables him to produce more of the same goods. This money now serves the production side. There it combines with individual ability, which is also a consequence of man's relation to spiritual life; and the degree to which individual ability has risen through schooling, self-education and experience determines the social form of production and its capacity for covering general needs. Such ability includes not only expert knowledge and technical skill, but moral qualities as well.

We see, then, that also by way of production the effects of spiritual life radiate into economic life. The producer owes the development of his productive talents to a free spiritual life, which in turn can cope effectively with its independent spiritual tasks only on the basis of a well-organized total economy; and the producer's will to serve economic life by furnishing an abundant (better put, "adequate"?) supply of

---

131 One wonders what Behrens would have made of Maslow's "hierarchy of needs" (1954). —Ed.

the social product will become stronger in proportion as he realizes this.

Insight into the function of purchase money awakens a sense of responsibility (in regard to "economic" work).[132] As a consumer, one will want to find the right measure in satisfying one's needs; and it will soon become manifest to one that this measure is determined by the sum of all those goods and achievements of labor, the consumption of which enables one to contribute one's own productive efforts to the total social product. Also, one will realize that a surplus of one's income is available as loan or gift-money.[133]

We believe we have shown that even the purely scientific concept "purchase money," with its relation to the concepts "loan money" and "gift money," throws light upon the true relation of the economic to the spiritual life, arousing the will to an ever more conscious shaping of this relation. In practice, such a conscious shaping would work out as a voluntary limiting of individual needs in order to reduce extravagance and the manufacture of goods that are economically and spiritually superfluous. The money and labor thereby saved could be made available for spiritual life in ever greater measure. This is the method by which, within the total social organism, an independent economic foundation could be laid for bringing forth great creations, notably monumental works of art, through spiritual activity. Unscrupulous economic exploitation of nature and the senseless waste of products manufactured out of her raw materials and forces would be replaced by careful cultivation and

---

132 CHB: Deleted: "the economic worker."

133 CHB: In this paragraph, in order to illustrate how readily one can get Behrens's analysis on a better track, "one" and "one's" have been replaced "he," "his" and "him."

transformation—a testimony to the awakening of the human spirit. The more thrifty economy is on the consumption side, the more lavishly can spiritual life unfold when munificence, in the creative sense, is in order.

The Position of the Rights Life in the Body Social

The relation of economic to spiritual life, however, cannot be wholly clarified without detailed characterization of a third social realm, which we have thus far only touched upon in passing. This is the domain of rights, out of which grows the state—meaning the political organization of a group of people who feel a certain affinity.

Only by recognizing the domain of rights as an independent sphere can its position within the social life be grasped in the right way. The social relationships established and developed within the rights life are totally different from those that unfold in economic or in spiritual life. In economic life, man as a producer enters into a relationship with nature by converting her products and raw materials into goods intended for consumption. His fellow men thereby become collaborators, and the work is divided according to individual capabilities. As a consumer, the human being is affected by nature, a fact suggested by the insistence of economic needs, and his fellow men thereby become fellow consumers. Thus, the total product of labor is distributed. However, man's relation to spiritual life lies in his individual contact with a higher world. In this respect, his social position is determined entirely by his spiritual achievements and the degree to which they are recognized by others.[134]

---

134 The more so if this recognition informs one's compensation. —Ed.

In the realm of rights, he stands in a very different relation to his surroundings. Here the essence of right acts as a socially constructive principle. The human mind has been at great pains to grasp this essence conceptually, especially since in recent times man's relation to nature, to human society and to his own being has become an enigma. One endeavors to throw light upon interrelationships of that sort by the employment of scientific observation and scientific thinking. There have been thinkers who have tried to explain right as something simply given with the nature of man: as though it were born not in him but with him. One would then merely have to research the nature of man in order to arrive at the nature of right. Thus, originated the doctrine of natural right. Another school of thought believes right to be an outgrowth of historical evolution, maintaining that the genesis and nature of right as it governed in the different epochs can be comprehended only through the study of history, particularly the history of law. And a third theory starts with the assumption that right is dependent upon the form of economic activity; that it has no independent being, but is determined by the changing and developing forms and exigencies of economic life. We cannot here enter into a detailed argument about such views, however; for our present purpose, which is limited to clarifying the relation between the economic and the spiritual life, the following general characterization of right must suffice.

In the first instance, the human being is not wholly conscious of his participation in the rights life. As a rule, he does not become aware of it until his feeling for right has been hurt by some injustice done to himself or to another. This feeling is still stronger when a man realizes that he himself has committed such an injustice. The feeling for right is based upon the ability to distinguish between good and evil, and it originates in the moral nature of man. An injury to one's sense of right furnishes an occasion for determining whether or not the rights life and within that the legal system, in which one is placed by destiny, is capable of rectifying the wrong done; and this is the point at which one becomes conscious of the existence of rights life, with its laws and methods of executing them. If the injured party finds it in harmony with his moral conceptions he will pronounce it good; if not, he will seek means for changing it.

A rights life in state form is one of the external conditions of existence into which the individual man is born. He simply encounters it as a realm of social life. It is something that has come into being historically. Law, on the other hand, and the political organization developing out of it, can come into being only through the cooperation of the members of a group, and for this reason it is not born with man. What is born in him, however, is the impulse to cooperate in changing and developing the legal system—and thereby also the form of state—if the existing laws and the methods of applying them no longer conform with the individual nature of man or with his relation to the economic and spiritual spheres. Such impulses cannot be called forth through a consideration of history; the human being must bring them to life within himself. History, and particularly the history of law, merely tells us how such impulses shaped the political life of the past, and did so, moreover, under totally different general conditions.

The direction taken by human development in the past becomes clear by comparing the attitude assumed today toward the existing rights life and state form with that taken by men of former epochs. Present-day man considers himself sufficiently mature to participate responsibly in shaping the rights life out of his own feeling for right. He desires to regulate his rights relations to his fellow men in cooperation with them and on a basis of equality. He attributes to every adult member of the group into which he was born the same capacity as his own for judging what shall be considered right and wrong. He feels "of age." This is the democratic impulse; and he who can experience it as a soul fact in its relation to the innermost core of human individuality—and as independent of any historical consideration—can also evaluate correctly the appearance of this impulse as a history-shaping force. Furthermore, he can understand the various forms assumed by the rights life and the state since the end of the Middle Ages. Antiquity and the Middle Ages become comprehensible as epochs that prepared the birth of the modern democratic impulse.

In ancient Greece and Rome originated the germ whose development made the form of the state, the constitution and laws the business of human personality. Previously, law had been a divine institution. Breaking the Law was tantamount to breaking with God. The Folk-God was a dictator in the literal sense of the term: his Word was the Law, carried out by his terrestrial representative, the king. On pictures in Egyptian temples one finds, as a rule, behind the Pharaoh the God inspiring him. In communities of pre-Antiquity, such legal and state systems as were formed out of the spiritual-religious life emphasized differences in status: *men were not equal before the Law. The idea of equality had not yet been born.* In the patriarchal system, the law was something different for man and woman, for father and son, for master and servant. Each caste was governed by different laws. An echo of this lives in Plato's *Republic*. This principle of inequality before the law becomes still clearer if we consider how, in the ancient cultures of pre-Antiquity rights were determined by blood. The descendants of one ancestor held no traffic with those of another. The principle of a social structure built upon blood-relationships excludes foreign blood. The differences in blood—that is, in tribes and races, and hence in peoples—is emphasized, and consequently also the inequality. This was carried to a point at which, even within a blood-community, purer blood took precedence over less pure in the granting of rights. The purer the blood, the nearer to the God, and therefore the greater the rights. The individual degree of god-likeness was decisive in law, not the general fact of human equality.

Not until the time of ancient Rome was a beginning made to do away with this principle of inequality: the Roman citizen came into being. Politically, he and his fellow citizens moved upon a plane of equality. He had emerged out of the old collective mentality and began to feel himself as a free personality[135] anxious to participate responsibly in shaping the rights life, the laws and the form of the state. Greek philosophical *thought* coupled with Roman political *will* led to the individualization of man and to the awakening of a spiritual freedom from which arose the idea of equality. The democratic idea made its appearance in human consciousness. By contemplating even the germ of democracy, which existed as far back as ancient Rome, it becomes clear that liberty and equality are not mutually exclusive, but that they

---

135 This is the time when the *persona* came about. —ED.

condition each other. Except that the idea of liberty must refer to the realm from which it arose and in which it must unfold: the spiritual realm. Liberation from the old spiritual fetters began in Antiquity. That which had been active in the old folk cultures as group-spirit now felt the urge to manifest itself in the matured individual, independent of the group. Man had become ready for the direct reception of the spirit, and thereby found himself in a new relationship to the being of his origin. This spiritual freedom had the effect of making him recognize, even in those of different bodily descent, a spiritual origin identical with his own. This recognition marks the beginning of the true democratic impulse in the realm of rights and of the state.

From the foregoing a further point becomes intelligible: when Antiquity had run its course, it found fulfillment in the impulse of Christianity. Through the Christ Event, spiritual freedom found its prototype in individual form as a quality, of man and of mankind: "I and the Father are one," a condition independent of blood and its laws achieved realization. This roused at the same time a feeling of equality: all men have their origin in the same Spiritual Father. For Christians, at any rate, nothing shows more clearly the spiritual origin of democracy than does the fact that, at the inception of Christianity, true equality was recognized in admitting every member of the community to Holy Communion.[136]

Although the democratic impulse did not come to practical expression in law and politics until after the end of the Middle Ages, it is quite impossible to understand its historical

136 CHB: Does this mean, conversely, that democratic behavior presupposes Christian behavior? If so, this would explain the doubtful nature of imposing Western democracy as if it were a universal truth, or judging non-Christian cultures in Christian terms.

development without recognizing its germ in Antiquity and its first individual embodiment in the Christ Event. The premise of such a historical understanding is man's immediate inner experience of the relation of his own freedom to the spiritual life. Part of this experience is a sense of his own individuality and of being surrounded by other individualities essentially of the same spiritual substance. To experience the nature of equality as a sun whose rays are caught by every man individually in his freedom and woven into his own being—that is what it means to experience democracy today. It can open the mind to an understanding of the historical Christ Event.

In moribund Antiquity, which became imbued with fresh folk forces flowing in from northern Europe, the Christ Event was the germ of a complete transformation of the social organism. This central impulse not only stimulates an ever-increasing individual experience of spiritual freedom and the recognition of general social equality, but is also active in bringing to life a comprehensive spirit of fraternity. Not only are men to feel themselves as matured individual children of one and the same Spiritual Father; they are to contrive, as brothers, a socially practical community life upon a new spiritual plane.

This idea of fraternity must be realized in the realm of economic life. It could not be realized in Antiquity because ancient culture, and in particular the rights life, were conditioned by an economic life taken care of by slaves; slavery was an institution sanctioned by public law. Not until medieval times did the effect of the Christian impulse bring about its abolition. The first beginnings of a metamorphosis of economic life appeared; and gradually it came to be based increasingly upon the ideal of cooperation between spiritually free men enjoying social equality. After the close of the Middle Ages this tendency became clearer and led to the progressive division of labor, the development of industrial production and the multiplication of ways and means of providing necessities. That the idea of fraternity, despite all antagonism and side-tracking, remains the true, organizing, ethical principle of economic life is shown by two phenomena:

1) the total social product, furnished through joint effort, is distributed in order to sustain life for all; and
2) labor is assigned according to the measure of individual capacity.

Fraternity is the health principle of economic life, and the recognition of this principle, although so inadequately put into practice, leads to the further insight that an unsentimental, matter-of-fact fraternity of this kind is possible only when economic activity is brought into proper relationship with the spiritual life. And this in turn is feasible only when the rights life can unfold in accord with its own nature as a mediator between spiritual and economic life. The state itself has no economic function, but is the upholder of rights that concern economy. It must neither establish nor administer the institutions of the spiritual life, but make and develop laws that guarantee the freedom of that life.[137] Only in this way can spiritual life evolve its own appropriate organization and administration.

---

137 CHB: The spirit at all times comes of itself, although premature, ill-timed or forced appearance may lead to it withdrawing or, more problematical, the entry into human affairs of an "inmate soul," to borrow the poet John Donne's phrase.

A rights life, for example, if it is to live up to the democratic impulse, will guarantee the security of personal property, in so far as this is justified by reasonable personal needs. It will protect the disposal of capital, or means of production, and real estate, as long as such property is administered in the general interest. Particularly will the state protect contracts between individuals and groups, provided they are entered into either in the general interest or in a justified individual interest. But a true rights state will not confiscate personal property for its own use, nor itself administer capital and means of production, nor bring about contractual settlements through its own initiative. (Other than necessary to its own conduct.) Furthermore, it will leave the organization and circulation of money to an associatively constituted economy, limiting its own function to the guaranteeing of the legal status of money as a public medium of exchange.[138]

In its relation to spiritual life the state will, for example, guarantee equal rights to all in education, in the opportunity to develop talent, and in acquiring membership in scientific, artistic, and religious institutions. But it will not administer such institutions itself, nor in any way influence education. Finally, a truly democratic state will find that its task consists in creating the technical conditions necessary for the proper functioning of an independent legal system, without, however, itself passing and executing judgment; for these are prerogatives of the spiritual sphere, which demands spiritual freedom.

A democracy can only be an organization of men with equal rights. It offers security on the one hand for a free

---

138 Is this not also a matter for associations? The state has no money and its upholding of contracts is enough to include compacts as to which currency is used in regard to them. —ED.

unfolding of spiritual life, and on the other, for both the fulfillment of economic contracts and the confining of economic
life within its own sphere. By fulfilling these tasks the state
does not acquire dominion over spiritual and economic life,
but rather it becomes the guarantor of their external security,
and thereby the mediator in their harmonious cooperation.
That is to say, the legal relation between economy and spiritual life, as set forth in this treatise, can be practically realized only when a truly democratic rights life is effectually
operative. Rudolf Steiner characterized the relationship of
these three members of the social organism in the following
words:

> In the free spiritual life, the individual will receive
> his social direction; in the independent rights life, the
> socially minded individual will engender the righteously
> effectual community will; and the socially informed
> individual wills, organized by the independent rights
> life, produce and distribute commodities in economic
> circulation according to social needs.[139] [It would be
> important to see the German for this!]

The Idea of the Threefold Social Order[140]

What has been described in the foregoing is an idea: the
idea of the threefold social order. It is a real idea, not one arbitrarily thought out. It is the formative reality of the social life
that is the true basis of its organs—that is, of all economic,
rights, and spiritual institutions. Heretofore in evolution—as
described here—this supersensible, form-building force has

---

139 *Spiritual Life, Civil Rights, Industrial Economy,* published by the
Anthroposophic Press, New York, CW 24, but originally published
in the *Hibbert Journal* 19:593 (1920)

140 See footnote 9.

been active without our having been fully conscious of it. Hereafter, however, it cannot work in the unconscious will or in the half-conscious feeling of man, because in these regions of the soul it has exhausted its progressive impetus. The time has come in which the idea of the threefold social order must be lifted out of the darkness of unconsciousness and the twilight of semi-consciousness into the full light of day consciousness. World history holds its breath, waiting to see whether man will recognize what the hour demands and voluntarily take the path of his destiny.

We are living in the scientific age whose impulse is to render conscious all that is now unconscious. This can be observed in every field. Physics, driven by the discovery of ever new phenomena, finds itself forced to move away from materialism and to recognize the activity of spiritual—that is, rational—agencies in the interrelationships of forces and matter. Biology is undergoing a change: it begins to regard the living organism as something based upon a supersensible form. Physiology turns more and more from the materialistic explanations of the 19th century to spiritual factors as causes of organic functions. It has rediscovered the unconscious mind as the widest and deepest region of soul-life and is trying to fathom its connection with the conscious. Sociology endeavors scientifically to comprehend the constructive and destructive forces in the social organism, in order to direct them in a purposeful way for the further development of social life; and in order to rescue the social organism from the rule of unconscious instinct it seeks to supplement its knowledge of the laws of nature with a knowledge of social laws. But all such endeavors must remain sterile hypotheses until such time as official science adds to its own methods those developed by anthroposophically informed spiritual science.

One result of such anthroposophical methods of research has been to bring to consciousness the idea of the threefold social order. This idea, if accepted by conscious volition, will give the social organism a form compatible with present conditions. At the same time, it becomes clear that all manifestations of spiritual decadence can be explained by the contradiction existing between deep-rooted habits of thought and the reality of life in the body social. A brief characterization, from this viewpoint, of the powers of obstruction and chaos will throw new light on the relation between the economic and spiritual spheres.

A superficial view sees the present organization of mankind as consisting of races, peoples and nations, linked through spiritual, political and economic ties. Within these groups live individuals similarly linked to individual members of the other groups. Now, that which lives side by side in *space* as races, peoples and nations, developed in *time*. Such groups, differing in physiological constitution, mentality and spiritual tradition, became what they are simply through historical development. Each group reached—or will reach—the apex of its culture at a certain point in time, which means the fulfillment of its task in history. Its leadership then passes to another group. It is a mysterious guidance of mankind, an activity of progressive forces. Thousands of years ago, this spiritual guidance made use of the people of India; then, successively, of the Persians, the Chaldean-Babylonian-Egyptian group of peoples, and then the Greco-Romans. This is a development that eventually led to the establishment of the Anglo-Germanic folk element as the foundation of the leading culture of our day.[141] As witnesses to the activity of the guiding impulse in epochs that antedated the Indian, we find cultures like the Chinese, or cultural remnants such as those on certain islands in the Pacific.[142] To understand the true nature of the social organism it is essential not to regard its historical development merely as something progressing smoothly in time to higher planes of existence. One must sense the struggle involved in conquering each new plane. The social organism is in continual conflict with forms of culture and civilization looming out of previous epochs. These act as a contradiction; and they encourage the organization of antiquated and selfish group interests at the very time when a universal relation between man and fellow man has become the decisive factor. The establishment of such a model relation between individuals in the fullness of consciousness is the task of Europe and its cultural extension, the United States.[143]

Not until true individualism—meaning not the continuation but the overcoming of egotism—has the strength to win through against and transform the artificially galvanized group spirits, can the task of culture be fulfilled. Group interests will continue to act as mutual enemies.

In the course of history, the human being has developed into a personality conscious of his own will; but as yet he has not raised this will from the level of egotism to true individualism. Consequently, not only does group oppose group at

---

141 By "Anglo-German," does Behrens mean Anglo-Saxon? What, in other words, does he understand "the leading culture of our day" to be? —ED.

142 The statement that Chinese and Polynesian cultures (what of Korean and Japanese?) predated Ancient India needs careful attention. —ED.

143 CHB: Europe: America. But what of Anglo-German, Anglo-American, and Anglo-Saxon?

the present time, but also the individual, throwing off tradition and old social obligations, opposes the social environment into which he was born. For his own selfish purposes, he seeks to exploit the historically developed institutions of spiritual life, rights life, and economic life, or to transform or even destroy them.

Thus, the causes of the chaos in which mankind finds itself today become clear. The social forms looming out of the past and conditioned by racial, folk, and nationalistic considerations seek to prevent the realization of a universal, democratic life, an effectual organization of world economy, and the freedom of the spiritual life; and the individual prevents the realization of a genuine social life, as Rudolf Steiner expresses it, "by silencing, in his thoughts and feelings, the depths of his being and thereby engendering within himself the impulse toward evil."[144]

The Role of Evil

These, then, are in the first instance the two sources of chaos: the group-spirit that has stood still in time, trying by

---

144 "Spiritual insight that penetrates to the essence of human nature finds there motives for action that are immediately good in the ethical sense as well. The impulse toward evil arises in us only because in our thoughts and feelings we silence the depths of our own nature. Accordingly, social ideas that are arrived at through the sort of spiritual concepts indicated here must, by their very nature, be ethical ideas as well. Since they are drawn not from thought alone, but from life, they possess the strength to take hold of the will and to live on in action. In true spiritual insight, social thought and ethical thought become one. And the life that grows out of such spiritual insight is intimately linked with every form of activity in human life—even in our practical dealings with the most insignificant matters" (Rudolf Steiner, *The Renewal of the Social Organism,* Steinerbooks, 1985. CW 24, pp. 6–7). Note, as the quotation shows, here Behrens has shifted gear, so much so that here we have introduced an extra subtitle, "The Role of Evil." —ED.

suggestion to force man into its centralistic special direction and to chain him to the past; and the individual who arbitrarily ignores the bounds set by the social demands of his day.[145]

Looking deeper, however, one discovers a third source of chaos. It is the impulse to combine the individual's forces of consciousness with the untransformed group instincts looming out of the past. In this case intellectuality, equipped with the methods and results of modern natural science and with a knowledge of economic organization and political propaganda, utilizes the group instincts for the purpose of realizing its own will to power. Then the groups emerge from their instinctive segregation and enter a war of mutual destruction.

To those able to penetrate more deeply, the powers of destruction have been perceptible as symptoms within the social organism for the last three or four hundred years; but these powers of destruction no longer work in secret. They have now openly made their appearance upon the stage of world-historical events, perceptible to the outer senses; perceptible even to the most external of the senses, the eye. An ever so dull and superficial observer who retains a modicum of judgment must recognize the existence of real powers of evil. For example, by means of nationally egotistical economies they have clearly prevented the formation of an organic world economy. Manifestly, a circumscribed economic life of this sort absorbs all spiritual forces for the task of raising a standard of living conceived in a purely materialistic sense; and it cannot be overlooked that such a spiritual life, lacking free air, renounces in self-emasculation the possibility of evoking those genuine

145 Here, mention is surely warranted of Rudolf Steiner's lecture course, *The Mission of Folk Souls* (CW 121). —ED.

human interests that transcend circumscribed group interests. In like manner, the conviction forces itself upon the observer of today that the power of evil prevents the state from creating out of its own being a rights life that will guarantee freedom for the spiritual life in the social realm, and the requisite security for economic life.

Rights life is the heart of the social organism, the center of the rhythm of social life, where extremes are balanced. The spheres of spiritual life and of economic interests find their proper social contact and equilibrium in the sphere of rights. But he who sees in the human heart only a pump will have no understanding of the heart of human society—rights. The state would become a machine receiving its impetus from egotistical economic and fanatical national interests, and would pump the water of life into those turbid channels where the spirit does not renew, vitalize and conserve, but where it ossifies, kills and destroys.[146]

It is characteristic of our time that the hidden causes of the disease of the social organism have become manifest in events—or, rather, non-events. It shows that these causes lie not so much in what men have done in the last three or four hundred years as in what they have left undone. They have failed to take cognizance of the basic idea of the social organism, and to socialize the individual will by receiving this idea as an ideal into their individual consciousness. This omission offered an opportunity for the entrance of powers that oppose this idea. Today, these powers have the liberty to kill and destroy, just as man has the same liberty to vitalize and build up. In other words, both good and evil have access to the boundless regions of liberty. The two sides of

---

146 Did Behrens mean: where the spirit is not renewed, vitalized and
    conserved, but where it is ossified, killed and destroyed? —ED.

existence, the light and the dark, have acquired equal opportunity for action, and the human being has the choice of identifying himself with one or the other. Potential freedom is the signature of our time. The choice of the free individual between good and evil is at the same time the fate of the social organism, and upon it hangs the life or death of human society. From its life will arise *terra lucida,* from its death *terra pestifera.*

The Call of the Spirit

An unprejudiced perception of the signs of our time sees certain aspirations connected with international matters in their true light. In all countries, there is an increasing demand for mutual understanding and for the bridging of racial and national contradictions upon a broad international basis. The motives behind this demand may spring from convictions of a general ethical nature—especially religious—or from scientific or political convictions; or again from the recognition of world-economic necessity. Propaganda is being spread for a more or less limited cooperation of peoples, by means of founding world institutions such as a new League of Nations, a Federal Union, or an International Supreme Court having an adequate police force at the disposal of its executive.[147]

In this way, conceptions move in the direction of a democratic super-state consisting not only of individuals but also of groups: of peoples and nations. One expects permanent peace from a super-state that would curtail the sovereignty of its members.

---

147 Children of Theodore Roosevelt's 1910 pronouncements? And, if so, antithetical to *The Mission of Folk Souls.* —Ed.

The model for this super-state would be provided by the parliamentary-bureaucratic state of today, which in a truly democratic sense is imperfect. But in this way all the inherent imperfections of present-day democracy would creep into the super-state. All contrasts of class and position, contradictions between young and old that result from a materialistic education and way of life, the inorganic tangle of spiritual life, rights, and economy, rashly applied technical methods, faulty investments—all these would be carried over into the super-state. In such an unlimited field their antisocial effects would be raised to an immeasurable degree. In place of the economic-minded, lopsided, dogmatic pressure groups of the present parliamentary national state, the nations themselves would organize into political parties and pressure groups. Each would seek to become a majority. The tendencies that lead to war would not be reduced but aggravated. Man himself, with his inherent relations to the spirit, to rights and to economy, would be devoured by such a super-political Leviathan hatched from a mating of selfish mass-madness and abstract mammoth planning.

The right path toward the establishment of a *supra-national*,[148] that is, universal organization of mankind will be entered upon only when speculative thinking ceases to take its point of departure from the planning of external institutions. It must start by accepting the true idea of an organism of mankind consisting of the three members as set forth. *Then a new type of thinking, inspired by this idea, will guide the individual will to the conscious evolution even of a supra-national organism.* In this same direction, appropriate institutions and their practical administration will come

---

148 CHB: That is, *not* a super-state.

into being. When the idea of the threefold ordering has been thoroughly understood as a demand of the present and has suffused our own attitude toward life, the supra-national community spirit will already have become socially active. It will have begun to organize. Conditions based on true confidence will have started to prepare the soil in which genuine spiritual relationships, truly democratic legal systems, and workable economic associations[149] can thrive. Institutions

---

149 BB: The term "economic associations," as employed by advocates of the threefold social order, does not imply the creation of something new. It refers, rather, to economic units that would result from the expedient transformation of organizations already existing. Modern economic life, based on industrialism, is a living organism whose members consist of association, and the formative forces of these arise out of the impulses that produce division of labor, cooperation, and the tendency to organize evinced by consumers and wholesale buying interests. But these forces that serve the associative principle cannot achieve full efficiency as long as the economy is thrown into chaos by lopsided and mutually antagonistic interests, growth of capital for its own sake, encouragement of the struggle inherent in competition and in the wage problem, political influence, and the attempt of government to bring about a centralized control of the economy. Corporations, cooperative concerns, companies, and individual enterprises of all sorts are, in fact, already economic associations, but under the threefold order the exclusion of the influences mentioned would transform them in a manner to permit an unobstructed and general application of the associative principle, which means the practical self-organization of economic and industrial organization free from state interference. Only in this way can the conditions be fulfilled under which the idea of a social organism, existing as a germ at the base of human history, can be realized as a universal social fact. An unprejudiced view of the true relation between the economic and cultural life and of the rights' task in purifying this relation paves the way for this event. The time required for such preparation will depend solely upon the strength and the persistence of the human will. He who follows the path indicated by Rudolf Steiner into the realm of supersensible reality, where the idea of the threefold social order waits for the prototype of mankind to be taken up into men's ego-consciousness, has begun to prepare its realization. He sees the world in a new light. In the chaos of the present he is the bearer and pioneer of the culture of the future.

with inexhaustible growing strength and adaptability could sprout from such soil.

An unencumbered spiritual life has through its very nature a universal human tendency toward the supra-national. An independent democratic legal order feels inherently impelled to recognize and protect general human rights, uninfluenced by national or other group interests. It is anthropocratic. An economic life organized according to its own conditions cannot do other than join an associative world economy.

10

Editorial Afterword

L ooking back on this project, one wonders at its eventual merit. It arose out of Fionn Meier's suggestion that, revisited today, Bernhard Behrens's legacy would give new life to the possibilities inherent in Rudolf Steiner's threefold conception of society—especially as this concerns the United States. Having now reviewed but also interrogated this legacy in detail and at some length, there is little doubt but that Fionn's intuition was valid. Only, the outcome is not perhaps what he anticipated. If judged not only by their seeming disappearance, but also his own postmortem anonymity, as first published, Behrens's booklets presumably had little effect. This is why, despite what some may experience to the contrary, I have sought to give them a kiss of life in my extensive footnoted critique. Although my comments may strike the reader at first as persistent criticism of a spoiling kind, I am confident that, read with, not against, Behrens's flow and intention, they will bring his contribution center-stage at this, very different, juncture in the destiny of the world and the role, or at least potential role, that the United States can play in it.[150] I feel no need to apologize for my remarks,

---

150 Written on the eve of what may well prove to be Donald Trump's
   second term as president. —ED.

therefore, insofar as they can be seen to be those of an Englishman accompanying a German in nudging the people of the United States—those concerned with the themes of this book, at least—onto truer and more viable tracks of "threefolding" in their country than have to date been possible.

Having shared my observations as much to clarify matters in my own mind as to provide a belated critique and update of Bernhard Behrens's own considerations (and so enter into conversation with him wherever he now is), at one point I thought to take them out or to combine them into this afterword. In the end, while aiming to ameliorate any disturbance by the device of light type, I opted for the hybrid solution of leaving them in place at the moments when and where the thoughts expressed arose but reviewing them in what follows. In that way, they can serve as a punctuation intended to run alongside Behrens's ideas, bringing them up-to-date, as it were, with world developments and, indeed, the evolution of associative economics since his day, the latter especially in link with accounting and financial literacy of an associative kind.

In what follows, I have used the standard social scientific practice of examining and exploring the "data" provided by my remarks in order to see what, if any, story they tell. I like to think this is in the spirit of Bernhard Behrens's own "methodical observation and cognition," although I know of it from Yin[151] and others, with whose late 20th-century work Behrens could not have been acquainted but probably would have appreciated. I have also done this mindful of a recent Bank of England chief economist, Andy Haldane, who (to paraphrase with some admittedly added Michael

---

151 Robert K. Yin, *Case Study Research: Design and Methods,* Sage, Thousand Oaks, CA, 1984.

eloquence) once said that there is no "news" in data as such; the reason for their collection and examination is to activate the researcher's intuitive mind, sensitizing it to insights that might be waiting or wanting to be born.[152]

Through the process, I have identified seven main themes, which I have then organized to tell their story, hoping in this way to bring this publication to a close with a sequence of topics that takes us from social scientific contemplation, with Rudolf Steiner's contribution fully embedded, to social scientific action:

1. Mono-discourse
2. Ethics
3. Rights
4. Some forks in the road of economics
5. Money and finance
6. Of Europe, Britain and America
7. United States history

Mono-discourse

First, the problem of a mono-discourse, a complaint often made when, in my experience, anthroposophists appear in the professional social scientific world—for example, a university or a central bank—knowing only what Rudolf Steiner had to say and unaware that he may not have been the only one to say anything. The result is that they look amateur, a disservice to Steiner who was better read than most and sought corroboration, not blind or untutored reiteration. In this way also, they fail to see which among Steiner's many insights are the real pearls, the contributions that are really new and not already known

---

152 Speaking at a memorial meeting for economist, Richard Roberts, Kings College London, Oct. 12, 2018.

in some, albeit ill-formed, way and in other terminology. The (valid) perception is then had of a contradictory mix of isolation from or unfiltered acceptance of modern social science on the part of many anthroposophists, along with their invention of ideas that are not truly scientific, neither socially nor spiritually.

The effect of all this is that, on the one hand, the world has been unable to benefit from Rudolf Steiner's contribution to the extent it might, and on the other, that little if anything of relevance or matching significance is expected. In this sense, as I noted, it is unfortunate that Behrens follows suit here in seeming to be unaware of the wider, especially Anglo-Saxon, discourse. Unfortunate, because, if there is to be hope of adoption and traction, the proponents of associative economics and threefold sociology need to be seen to arise within and belong to that world, not addressing, let alone preaching to, it from outside.

Ethics

Second, there is the general area that I have called ethics, which needs to be as ecumenical as possible, insofar as socioeconomic evolution, while it may, as an image at least, eventually entail humanity-wide membership of the Anthroposophical Society, will not start out that way. It will begin in ecumenical anonymity, as it were, one of the many chambers in the Father's house. Rather than being conditional, its essential Christianity has somehow first to be experienced raw and unworded. That means also that a tendency to moralizing, what Steiner once referred to as the use of "moralic acid," has to cede the stage of economics to more objective, but nonetheless concretely spiritual considerations. Hence, my suggestion that the prior notion of self-discovery should preempt any sense of religiosity or soul invasion that words like "self-development" and "self-mastery" risk implying. This is above all necessary if one wishes to overcome, not just confront, the positivism that informs much of modern social science, especially economics.

In particular, this requires the refusal of any spiritual elitism that accompanies and derives from frequently speaking as if spiritual life is superior to rights and economic life. We must rid ourselves and our lexicon of the nuance of spiritual life having a higher or special status, as if only some people belong or exist there, rather than it being one of the three spheres of society, which the I has to bring into their right relationship. In the same vein and inwardly connected, we need to avoid the classification of society into groups or classes, rather than entrepreneurs of various types and propensities. For this, we must find ways to posit, not only the possibility, but the fact of ethically individual entrepreneurs and of associations as their professional counterpart and manner of self-conduct; as the province of entrepreneurs "when not acting egotistically." For to whom else can a self-governing economy be entrusted?

Not to meet this challenge is to court another, much more serious problem: of being an accomplice to the inculcation of an inmate spirit in the study and conduct of economic affairs, such as one may describe today's primarily Samuelsonian ethos. It is not enough to bemoan the vale of tears in which we find ourselves, we have also to beat the pathway out of it. In a nod to this anniversary year of the World Power Conference, this is something that Daniel Dunlop said was a matter of knowing the gods' and one's own timing.

But also knowing where the forks in the road lie hidden and, therefore, wrong turnings are possible. Such as misreading sacrifice. Get that wrong, and the whole history underlying Anglo-Saxon evolution is ill-conceived, also by its proponents. It is not even, as I have argued in my critique, that surplus is a matter of excess will forces, not sacrifice; the misinterpretation of sacrifice on moral rather than economic grounds hides something else—the sacrifice of egotism, the steering of one's will into paths that serve others, not oneself.

Rights

Predictably, the topic of rights can be a very touchy one because one first has access to it through one's sense of right, something deeply intimate to one's karma and not, therefore, readily found as common ground. On this matter, I only want to aver that I think one has to go very carefully when suggesting that there can be worldwide rights, rather than rights boundaried by the country (rather than nation) one finds oneself in. This is an allusion to folk souls, to the distinction between archangels and archai, countries and the world as a whole; as also between their "good" and "bad" versions. It may be the Anglo-Saxon in me, but I would first seek harmonization of rights on the world stage rather than the formation of rights valid for all countries, such as happens when the European Union, for example, displaces the rights life of countries that would adhere to it. In Behrens's argument, it seems to me enough to say that democracy is an ideal everyone can relate to without the form of its institutions being identical. This is why, in world economic life especially, I aver multilateral arrangements over supernational ones, and also why, probably, the governments of the United States persistently prefer the opposite!

Some Forks in the Road of Economics

In economics in general, there are other forks in the road, places where one can take a wrong turn. A very real case in point is Steiner's distinction between Values 1 and 2—in his words, value created by labor transforming nature and value created by spirit organizing labor. Beware creating two classes of people at this point, or thinking the one can occur without the other. Spiritual elitism finds its entry here, suggesting that teachers are superior to cobblers, when in fact teachers, if they are employees (which most are, also in Waldorf schools) rather than self-governing entrepreneurs, are arguably of a lesser status than those who make or mend our shoes on a basis of initiative and financial sovereignty.

It is especially important not to think one can transform nature, or grow food other than by giving expression to one's capacities, albeit in service to others, not oneself. The tyranny of "land" over "capital" is as dangerous in our movement as it is prevalent. There is no denying that "land" is the ground on which we stand, but it is we who step onto it.

Likewise, beware splitting "labor" into two—its organization and its application. It is of the essence of being human that one, everyone, should take hold of him- or herself, of his or her talents, destiny and lives-long journey in service to others. Once we have outgrown *ex cathedra* statements and sentiments, how else do we grow into and know our humanity? The world needs to be conceived as one that hallows work in this sense, rather than shuns or shirks it. For this, but nowhere mentioned by Bernhard Behrens as it happens, true prices are the watchword—as well as bringing about a world in which they obtain.[153] On this depends living from income not capital, revenue not savings. As also on the recognition of one's humanity and the associated dignity implicit on being paid an amount of money commensurate with what one intends to do or produce, not what one has done or produced. This, rather than a life of subsistence revenue that drives one into stock markets and other instruments, not in order to capitalize others, but in order to have them provide an unworked for income for oneself. Indeed, if truth be known, at this stage in economic history, paying one another true prices would be the epitome of fine actions, bringing a smile to Aristotle's lips, then or even now.

Money and Finance

And so one enters ineluctably into that most spiritual of domains: modern finance, meaning finance from which egotism has been "extirpated root and branch." To say this is to address modern financialization head-on, the very process that recent economic development, especially that of the 19th and 20th centuries, has taken as its foundation. If we are to get beyond the conditions into which this has led us, we have to do so by systematically revising the very concepts and related policies and institutions that it has given rise to: and which for the most part became the substance of

---

153 He does, however, treat this topic in *Anthroposophically oriented Economics*, see footnote 1. —ED.

what is now taught in economics and business administration classes the world over. The list is specific, if embarrassing and awkward.

The application of capital, for example, has to pass from those who own it to those who use it, and in accordance with the latters' terms and circumstances. They, however, have also to be financially literate. This is the secret to the otherwise strange-sounding Western adage: never do business with your own money. As also why in the United States the "true" economic spirit is of "self-made" people who "make money," rather than relying on what their forbears or others have done. In Steiner's terms, this means giving life, not just lip service, to the idea of "personal credit," eschewing lending to assets rather than individuals (i.e., collateralizing lending), or trusting one's extra money to anonymous corporations rather than the bakery or school next door.

We also need to desist our egotistical use of such things as the distinction between stocks and bonds, and let go the convenient but ill-conceived fiction that those who risk their capital should get the reward of whatever is left over. The capital at risk in an associative economy is the capital that fails to flow on, not the capital that fails to "come back." The risk is that an insight or an initiative belonging to the future will be blocked by the preservation rather than circulation of capital and the means of production from the one capable person or generation to the next—and as a matter of direct, not purchased right.[154] In such a world, the related conventions of "returns" and "savings" all wait to be replaced by associative economic, not banking, precepts and behavior. Above all, now is the time

---

154 Excluding the nominal "consideration" often required to substantiate a transfer of rights. —Ed.

when everyone, if true-price-remunerated, should be able to identify wealth in excess of his or her requirements and learn to pass that wealth on to where it can be made fruitful for and by others. Surely, it does not take clairvoyance to see how one's possession of capital can easily become one's possession by capital.

Of Europe, Britain and America

By this pathway, we are quietly entering into the story of Europe and America, so-called—that place destined to become known as the United States, a refuge for many and the location of the "American dream." Just as Europe in its true sense represents the place of humanity in microcosm, so the United States is the scene or stage on which that humanity has to come to terms with all from which it was protected in pre-Columbus times: the forces of materialism and the soul challenges these entails, but also the soul triumphs possible when they are comprehended and mastered. A place, too, of course, in which those running from autocracy and despotism were running to a constitution born of the long evolution of Saxon governance, emerging out of its pre-Witan development, through Magna Carta and parliamentarianism, superimposed on or having usurped Iroquoian constructs, to result in a republic that, though proud of itself, struggles to inhabit and do justice to the promise of such an appellation. And a place where the social and even physical architecture of Roman times strangely reappears.

That, or so it would seem, is what Behrens expects. Because he does not see the foundation of the United States in the mores of other cultures or corners of history. And that despite, or perhaps precisely because of, his reference to Goethe, the Goethe who sought "a favorable destiny beyond the seas." And yet, to my mind, Behrens errs here in seeing the proletariat as the fourth rather than third estate made up of peasants and artisans herded and trapped in factories. The error is a double one, moreover, because it occludes perception of the fourth estate as the I, the very "instrument" by which threefold society is to be experienced and made a reality.

On this, in turn, depends his failure to address clearly the difference between Anglo-German, Anglo-American and Anglo-Saxon. Are these synonymous or do they have different stories to tell? Arguably, *Anglo-Saxon* underlies *Anglo-German*, not only because of those peoples' shared Saxon heritage, but because, per Behrens, the English and the Germans are cousin peoples, and would have remained so had, according to him, the Germans not lost their mission (as also did the English, of course).

Anglo-American, on the other hand, surely refers to something else: namely, the "special relationship" between those who not only have English as their mother tongue, but share what one might call a predilection for lodge behavior, and with that a tendency to place the English-speaking peoples above all others. Here, as I understand it, one enters the super-delicate subject of outright, if unspoken, opposition to Rudolf Steiner's ideas inasmuch as those ideas, by their nature rather than their intent, are the opposite of those required to rule the world and all who inhabit it. They admit to no hegemon but the human I, when endowed with as much consciousness of itself as it can be in our times.

How this plays out currently and imminently in terms of the United States' perception of itself and as seen in associative economic and threefold terms remains to be seen. But one needs to hazard something of how this might be envisaged if one is to lead Bernhard Behrens's hopes and expectations, such as he was able to express them in the early 1950s, out into the world—and the United States—as it now stands. Why else, would one republish his works and do so with gusto and serious intent?

Strange to relate, a key here is not to replace Great Britain with "UK" (for United Kingdom), for then one loses sight of post-imperial Britain, of what it could have gone on to do or become, especially when one looks at the work of Keynes and Steiner. In particular, if one never imagines how a worldwide proto-global empire could have become translated into a worldwide commonwealth of countries collaborating (but not united together politically) in the conduct of a single associative global economy. Nor does one notice the subtle way in which "great" was misread by all concerned as grandiosity, politically and imperially great rather than geographically greater. Or how the concept of uniting nations is thereby insinuated into history—in this case, the, still problematical, uniting of the English, Scots, Welsh and Irish.

Here is not the place to elaborate on the history that has been overshadowed by events since 1914, but it is the place to observe that replacing Great Britain with United Kingdom is a trick of the English language. It also falsely suggests the subsuming of Britain into the United States, at the same time quietly denigrating the role of constitutional monarchy, when in fact that was never the real *casus belli* of the American Revolution.

To mention all this is to draw attention to the tip of a very large iceberg (historical pun not intended), deep investigation of which, however, will likely lead to what it lies in the future of the United States to do—and the rest of the world for that matter. That, in turn, will depend on how we understand the history to date of that part of the planet destined to be occupied by the United States.

U.S. History

Again, neither space nor time permit detail. Suffice it to say, that one has to go back to the "First Nations" and what was extant spiritually, politically and economically before the settlers (of various stripes, but especially those with founding and religious intent) arrived from Europe. And to what they had been protected from prior to the discovery—better put, uncovery—of that region at the dawn of the modern, consciousness soul, era. What did Bernhard Behrens have in mind when speaking of "virgin soil," for example—the actual land area or the spiritual ground?

On such an enquiry, including the role of Templars, true Rosicrucians, Freemasons and so on, will depend our constitutional comprehension going forwards. What really is in the heady mix of repudiated monarchy, confederate principles, centralized political power and messianic global pretensions? How can the threads of such an entanglement be disentwined? And were one able to do so, would one find only the three—spiritual, rights and economic—or something more complex? And if only the three, are they ripe for conscious formulation and institutional representation?

By that I mean, when elaborating the "theory" of three-fold society and associative economics, what is one to do with such current institutions as the Federal Reserve System, income taxation, the state's capture of gold, a finance-infested bi-party political system, and so on—not to mention the European Union, the European Council, NATO, the IMF, World Bank, and WTO, etc.?

Of today's institutions, can one identify and differentiate between those that belong to the image Steiner shared of a threefold society and a single associative world economy, those that are caricatures of that, those that are in naïve opposition to it, and those that are the bearers of inmate forces? To paraphrase the three aims of the United States to which Behrens drew our attention, is this how we will find the way to bring democracy to everybody, affording a permanent basis for peace and opening the way for the spirit to manifest through free individuality?

To my mind, it belongs to the merit of Bernhard Behrens's work, once brought up to date and, as I put it, "tidied up," that it can help set our sails fair for such a coming wind, assuming the Gods intend it and that we are fit enough as sailors to catch it. Whether that wind will blow fresh from behind because we better understand what the United States is all about, or new from in front, because that understanding allows us to see more accurately what lies before us, remains to be seen. But in that event, the "us" would refer to all those for whom, as the venue for all humanity to meet and master its untrammeled but also unbridled will, the United States is a shared country.

www.ingramcontent.com/pod-product-compliance
Lightning Source LLC
Chambersburg PA
CBHW020244290326
41930CB00038B/348

9 7 8 1 6 2 1 4 8 3 8 1 6